ACHIEVEMENT IN MATHEMATICS

ACHIEVEMENT IN MATHEMATICS

DIGUMARTI BHASKARA RAO
DIGUMARTI PUSHPA LATHA

DISCOVERY PUBLISHING HOUSE
NEW DELHI—110 002

Published by:

DISCOVERY PUBLISHING HOUSE PVT. LTD.
4383/4B, Ansari Road, Darya Ganj
New Delhi-110 002 (India)
Phone : +91-11-23279245; 23253475; 43596065
E-mail : discoverybooksindia@gmail.com
discoverypublishinghouse@gmail.com
namitwasan9@gmail.com
web : www.discoverypublishinggroup.com

First Published: **1995**

Reprinted: **2022**

ISBN: 978-81-7141-278-5

Achievement in Mathematics

Printed at:
Infinity Imaging Systems
Delhi

Preface

Mathematics is the abstract science which investigates deductively the conclusions implicit in the elementary conceptions of numerical and spatial relations. It is a systematized and organized science, it is a science of logical reasoning, and it is also a language of mankind.

Mathematics is one of the languages of human life and certainly no more marvellous language was ever created by the mind of man. Mathematical language cut short the lengthy statements through its symbols, it is free from verbosity, it helps the expression of ideas in an exact form, and it enables to understand and appreciate precision, brevity, sharpness, logic and beauty of mathematics.

Mathematics is studied as pure mathematics and applied mathematics. Pure mathematics involves systematic reasoning, concerns only to theories and principles without regard to their application, consists of all those assertions as that if such and such proposition is true of any thing and such and such another proposition is true of that particular thing, and is developed on an abstract, self-contained basis without any regard to any possible kind of practical applications that may follow. Applied mathematics is the application of pure mathematics in the service of a specific or given purpose. It has practical applications to the natural phenomena, it has a lion's share in the development of different disciplines, and it is a connecting link between pure mathematics on one side and physical, biological, social and technical sciences on the other.

Mathematics fulfils the educational values such as practical, disciplinary, cultural, intellectual, moral, vocational, aesthetic, social, inter-disciplinary, etc.

Identifying the role of mathematics in life and education, the researchers are interested in studying the achievement in mathematics of +2 students. This particular sample is selected because the achievement at this stage plays a major role in getting admission into professional courses.

The achievement, on the whole, is high at +2 level. The students studying in residential colleges have achieved well than their counterparts. The boys are also superior than girls in their achievement in mathematics.

The sample selected is from an educationally advanced geographical area. There is also much competition between residential and non-residential colleges with regard to teaching, training, facilities and achievement. The conditions that are prevailing in residential colleges must be extended to non-residential colleges, as far as possible to make students come out with flying colours.

Dr. Bhaskara Rao
Mrs. Pushpa Latha

Acknowledgements

We are thankful to

Mrs. Chennupati Sridevi, *Guntur*
Mr. David Bergamini, *U.S.A.*
Prof. Talvi Marja, *Estonia*
Prof. Arild Tjeldvoll, *Norway*
Prof. Marlown Ediger, *U.S.A.*
Prof. Evelin Witruk, *Germany*
Prof. Skip Hills, *Canada*
Prof. Ake Bjerstedt, *Sweden*
Prof. Brian McAndrews, *Canada*
Prof. Kiyoshi Amano, *Japan*
Dr. B.K. Manmohan Singh, *Hyderabad*

for their academic co-operation

Bhaskara Rao
Pushpa Latha

Contents

Introduction

Mathematics is the science of spatial and numerical relationship. Probably pre-historic man learned to count on their fingers. The Chinese, Hindus, Babylonians and Egyptians devised the methods of counting and measuring. The first theoretical mathematicia is held to be Thales of Miletus, who is believed to have proposed the first theorem in plane geometry. His disciple, Pythagoras established geometry as a recognized science among the Greeks. The later School of Alexandrian geometry included Euclid and Archimedes. Our present decimal numerals are based on a Hindu-Arabic system which reached Europe from Arab mathematicians of the near-east. Geometry was revitalized by the invention of co-ordinate geometry by Descartes, and Pascal and Fermat developed probability theory. Napier invented logarithms and Newton and Leibniz developed calculus. In Russia, Lobachevsky rejected Euclid's parallelism and developed non-Euclidean geometry. Much early matrix theory was developed by a British mathematician, Arthur Cayley, although the term was first coined by his contemporary James Sylvester. Today, higher mathematics has a powerful new tool, the mig-speed electronic computer, which can create and manipulate mathematical 'models' of various systems in science, technology and commerce. Modem methods of teaching arithmetic involving sets are sometimes referred to as 'new maths'.

Attempts to define so broad a subject as mathematics have not been very successful. Benjamin Peirce, one of the best of the America-trained mathematicians, said that "Mathematics is the science that draws necessary conclusions". Such a definition trespasses upon the domain of logic but there are many who would relate logic and mathematics, as sciences more closely than is commonly done. Professor Bocher has suggested a basis of definition. "we may seek some hidden resemblance in various objects of mathematical investigation and having found an aspect common to them all, we may fix of this as the one true object of mathematical study, or we may abandon the attempt to characterize mathematics by means of its objects of study, and seek in its methods its distinguishing characteristics. Finally there is the possibility of combining these two points of view". When, however, we attempt to define the science with respect to its objects, we are confronted by so many difficulties that there seems but little hope of success. There seems more chance of favourable results in attempting to define the science by means of methods and numerous efforts, in this direction, have been made. Professor J.W. Young has recently suggested the definition of "Abstract mathematical system" as a system of symbols devoid of content except such as is implied in the assumptions concerning them, and then saying that "Mathematics as a whole might then be defined as that consisting of all such abstract mathematical systems together with all their concrete applications". These attempts at defining the mathematical science serve atleast to show the broadening of the subject from century to century.

Mathematics is one of the most useful and fascinating divisions of human knowledge. It includes many topics of study. For this reason, the term 'mathematics' is difficult to define. The term "mathematics" comes from a Greek word meaning "inclined to learn".

Most of the basic mathematics taught in school involves the study of number, quantity, form and relations. Arithmetic, for example, concerns problems with numbers. Algebra involves solving equations in which letters represent unknown quantities. Geometry concerns the properties and relationships of figures in space.

Computing is solving mathematicals problems that involve much work with numbers. A computer is a mathematical machine that performs calculations at a very high speed. Mathematicians use computers to perform complex calculations in a few minutes that would take thousands of years with a pencil and paper.

The most important skills in the mathematics are careful analysis and clear reasoning. These skills can help people to solve some of the deepest puzzles. Mathematics is based upon logic. Starting from widely accepted statements, mathematicians use logic to draw conclusions and to develop complete mathematical systems.

DEVELOPMENT OF MATHEMATICS

Mathematics is not so much a body of knowledge as a special kind of language, one so perfect and abstract that—hopefully—it may be understood by intelligent creatures throughout the universe, however different their organs of sense and perception. The grammar of the language—its proper usage—is determined by the rules of logic. Its vocabulary consists of symbols, such as:

numerals for unknown numbers;

letters for unknown numbers;

equations for relationships between numbers;

π for the ratio of the circumference to the diameter of a circle; sin (for sine), cos (for cosine) and tan (for tangent) for the ratios between sides in a right triangle;

$\surd$ for a square root;

∞ for infinity;

Σ, $\int$, ∂ and $\rightarrow$ for assorted other concepts in higher mathematics.

All of these symbols are tremendously helpful to the scientist because they serve to short-cut his thinking. To many laymen, however, they make mathematics seem less a universal language than a massive linguistic barrier between the so-called "two cultures" of modern society, represented by the scientists and the humanists.

Only part of the vocabulary of mathematics has been preempted by science. The rest of it—and all of the grammar—remains in the sphere of general human thought. Indeed, mathematics has as much to do with philosophy, economics, military strategy, musical composition, artistic perspective and parlor games as it as to do with atomic physics. Because of its virtuosity, anyone well taught in it can love it with the same warmth that a devotee feels for the ballet, fine silver, antiques or any other adornment of civilization.

In view of its esthetic aspect and its total unconcern with practicality, pure mathematics may seem the most pointless pursuit ever devised by dreamers. But even branches of mathematics which only recently were deemed utterly useless are today vitally important to industrialists, generals and government planners. Our civilization would scarcely exist without the physical laws and intellectual techniques developed as by product of mathematical research. No one can balance his checkbook without applying arithmetic invented by the ancient Mesopotamins and Hindus. No one can build a wall without drawing on techniques of geometric measurement developed by Egyptian mathematicians. It was Greek pioneers of geometry who conceived the idea that the earth might have the shape of sphere. Classical mathematics, when rescued from the oblivion of the dark Ages, helped ignite the adventurous spirit of the era of Columbus. The men who wrought the Industrial revolution gained confidence in machines and what they could do from the partly mathematical, partly scientific investigations of Galileo and Newton. Today, atomic research draws heavily on Einstein's Theory of Relativity, which in turn utilized abstruse 19th century algebraic speculations.

The two pillars of mathematics in antiquity were arithmetic, the science of numbers, and geometry, the science of shapes and spatial relationships, Over the centuries arithmetic was augmented by algebra, which provide a shorthand notation for doing arithmetic when unknown quantities were involved. In the 17th Century, arithmetic and algebra were unified with geometry in "analytic geometry," which provided a technique for mapping numbers as points on a graph, for converting equations into geometric shapes and for converting shapes into equations. The analytical approach of this new geometry, clarifying one branch of mathematics in terms of another, opened the way to most of the disciplines of higher mathematics—disciplines which are encompassed by the single word "analysis"..

The first offspring of analysis was calculus, a system for analyzing change and motion in terms of points or numbers strung together in continuous sequences. This enables scientists to solve problems in dynamics—to understand the ripple of a wave, the arc of a shooting star, indeed all the simpler fluctuations of nature. Calculus remains a standby for technologists when they design ears and aim rockets.

Many scientist believed, when calculus first came into use, that it would ultimately let them predict the continuing behavior of every moving thing. But at about the same time, through studying gambling games, mathematicians discovered the laws of probability, which reminded them of the leaven of uncertainty that lurks in almost any sequence of events. Today such laws help set the rate a 50-year-old man must pay on a new insurance policy. They enable pollsters to estimate, from any given sampling of voters, the chances of making an accurate election forecast. And they are used in atomic experiments, to evaluate statistically the buckshot patterns which millions of invisible subatomic particles make when they strike a target at the muzzle end of an atom smasher.

By means of vastly complicated equations evolved out of calculus and analytic geometry, mathematicians conceived of geometric shapes beyond our visual ken—shapes of more than the ordinary dimensions of height, width and depth, shapes with any number of dimensions. They also conceived of infinitely dimensioned spaces to put the shapes in. The concept of more-than-three-dimensional spaces has become basic to ideas about relativity and the universe. It has also led to solutions for difficult problems about electrical and magnetic fields in the complicated gadgetry of computers and television sets. At the present time practitioners of geometry are pursing a still further abstraction of their art through "topology," the art of analyzing those properties of a shape which remain unaffected after the shape itself has been shrunk, stretched or twisted.

Other mathematicians have reached back to find inspiration in the most elementary mathematical ideas of all. The "number theorists" have returned to the deceptively simple steps we count by, and repeatedly they have concluded that the integers, or ordinary whole numbers—one, two, three and on up—are the most baffling, stimulating and enter training of all mathematical subjects. Even the underlying processes of thought itself have become a target for mathematical probes. The meanings of the nouns and the verbs used in ordinary human reasoning, mathematicians say, are subject to different interpretations; why not replace them with symbols as unambiguous as numerals and with operations as unambiguous as addition and multiplication? Proponents of this "symbolic logic" have brood on ways of reducing all objects of human study to "sets" and "groups"—collections of thoughts or things that go together logically, such as "all blue eyes" or "all women drivers." And they have tried to find strictly logical ways of making non-odious comparisons by matching elements in one set or group with those in another.

The varieties of mathematics sketched above constitute its main mountain ranges. Innumerable spurs and foothills fringe these ranges. Geometry's many branches include projective, affine, Euclidean and Riemannian; algebra's include Banach, Boolean and homological. All these ingenious creations of thought not only have application in everyday life but in fundamental way also spring from life. When an Amazon Indian blows a poisoned dart at a monkey in treetop, he intuitively judges a missile trajectory that could be more exactly judged by analysis and the laws of motion. When you step on the gas to pass a car, you risk your life on an estimate that can be made precise through calculus.

Today there is hardly any human activity or thought process—from hunting enemy submarines to composing music—which mathematicians have not sought to reduce to its essential elements. As a result mathematics has kept growing. Its great works are repeatedly rewritten and put in more symmetrical, general, precise and useful terms. This unending revision has helped to keep mathematics—even after some 6,000 years of development—from becoming impossibly bulky and sprawling. Until about a century ago, a gifted mathematician could still hope to master all of it in some detail. Even now a student can get a fairly representative bird's-eye picture of the whole in order to choose a specialty.

While both teaching techniques and problem-solving in mathematics can often be simplified, the abstract fundamentals can never be made easy. About 2,300 years ago, it is said, Ptolemy I asked the Greek mathematicians Euclid for a quick explanation of geometry. The answer was tart: "There is no royal road to geometry." Euclid's answer still holds good, and for all branches of mathematics. The professionals who have traveled the road naturally feel a mixture of superiority and helplessness toward all the inquiring modern Ptolemies who would like to make a jet-paced conquest of the whole terrain.

Fortunately, just as it is not necessary to become fluent in the language of a country in order to appreciate the character of its people, so it is not necessary to be able to say

$$\lim_{\Delta\chi_i \to 0} \sum_{i=1}^{m} f(\chi_i)\Delta\chi_i$$

to a mathematician—or even to pronounce it properly—in order to appreciate the main branches of his subject, to know what they are about why they are exciting and valuable, and how they have come into being.

Mathematics began with the invention of numbers to count by. Prehistoric man's need to count at all was limited, if we can judge by his latter-day kin, the surviving Stone Age tribesmen of Australis. New Guinea and Brazil. Many do not have names for numbers beyond 2 or 3. No doubt part of the reason is that they live in small family groups and are poor in possessions. Probably, too, they have few words to represent whole groups of things which might be counted. Some of them, for instance, are instinctive botanists who can recognize and name hundreds of separate species of trees but have no general word for "tree" itself. A Brazilian Indian chief is likely to react with scorn to the question "How many"? If pressed, he can usually summon a special medicine man—anthropologists actually call the man a "numerator"—to invent compound-number names out of 1s, 2s and 3s, and to recite them ceremoniously after each possession the chief may list.

When the glaciers retreated about 10,000 years ago, some nomadic Stone Age hunters in the hill country of the Middle East evolved a new way of life: farming. At once they faced the problems of keeping track of days and seasons, and of knowing what quantities of food grain and seed grain to store. As more complex agricultural societies developed in the valleys of the Nile, Tigris and Euphrates, the farmer confronted a further problem: paying taxes. All these prerequisites of civilization required that numbers be given names and that counting be elaborated beyond the primitive notions of "one" and "many".

Some ancient tribes, it is believed, used a base of 2 to count by : 1, 2, 2-1, 2-2, 2-2-1 and so on. Others used a base of 3: 1, 2, 3, 3-1, 3-2, 3-3, 3-3-1 and so on. As they became farmers and builders, the most advanced peoples pushed their basic counting limit higher. Many used their own fingers and toes as the handiest counters, thus amassing new numbers all the way up to 20—at which point fingers and toes ran out. Early 20-based number systems are still remembered in the French words for 80 and 90.

"quatre-vingt" and "quatre-vingt-dix," which mean "four-twenty" and "four-twenty-ten," and in the 20-shilling pound of old British monetary system. The traditional British system, with its ha'pennies, pennies, threepence, sixpence, shillings, half crowns, pounds and guineas, was a ½-1-3-6-12-30-240-252 system—a mixture of several archaic systems.

Whatever the system they used for counting, the merchants of the early civilizations presumably used pebbles piled up on the ground to represent the numbers counted. It was probably out of such a method that we acquired the computing device known as the abacus, which is still standard equipment in bazaars from Tehran to Hong Kong. The abacus may have begun as sort of poker pot in which a certain kind of chip would stand for 1, another for 10, another for 100. Eventually, varieties of the abacus were evolved. Some were mechanically organized so that the one-chips slid on one bar, the ten-chips on another, the hundred and ten-hundred chips on a third and fourth. By flipping these counters up and down, the ancient trades could add and subtract faster than most people can with pencil and paper today.

The skillful use of tally-tokens for handling financial calculations may have retarded the perfection of written numbers. And it was from the development of written notations for numbers that modern arithmetic and modern algebraic ideas were to grow. One of the crudest ways of writing numbers is preserved for us in the Roman numerals I, II, III, IV, V, VI and so on. Essentially this is a technique in which every number is expressed as the addition or subtraction of a few basic symbols. We use a similar system when we keep a score by /, //, ///, ////.

It is believed that the written symbols for numbers which we use today—1, 2, 3, 4, 5, 6, 7, 8 and 9— originated with the Hindus. They were devised to go with a 10-based, or "decimal," method of counting, so named after the Latin word decima, meaning tenth, or tithe. The way we put our numbers together seems simple enough, but it is in fact the artful product of centuries of development—what the mathematicians call a "positional notation." In this system the position of each digit in a sequence of numerals decides its value. The numbers larger than 1 are separated from the numbers smaller than 1 (the fractions) by a decimal point. To the left of the point, the first digit is worth just itself: the next digit is worth itself times 10; the next digit, itself times 100; the next digit, itself times

1,000, and so on. To the right of the decimal point, the first digit is worth 1/10 of itself; the next digit, 1/100 of itself; the next digit, 1/1,000 of itself, and so on.

The number 8,765,4321, for example, means $8 \times 1{,}000 + 7 \times 100 + 6 \times 10 + 5 \times 1 + 4 \times 1/10 + 3 \times 1/100 + 2 \times 1/1{,}000 + 1 \times 1/10{,}000$. Ultimately a shorthand device was invented, the so-called "power," or "exponent," by which the number 8,765.4321 can also be expressed as $8 \times 10^3 + 7 \times 10^2 + 6 \times 10^1 + 5 \times 10^0 + 4 \times 10^1 + 3 \times 10^2 + 2 \times 10^3 + 1 \times 10^1$. In the case of 10^3, the number 3 indicates the "power," and is another way of signifying 10×10×10, or 1,000, Similarly, the negative exponents are used to denote the decimal fractions. Thus, 10^3 means $1/10^3$ or 1/1,000 or 0.001.

Within this system of powers, a question sometimes arises as to the meaning of 10^0, or 10 to the zero power. From our 8,765.4321 sequence, it will be apparent that 10^0 lies between 10^1 and 10^1, or between 10 and 1/10 and it is defined as equal to 1. This neat symmetry of powers extends to other numbers besides 10, and except for zero itself, every number raised to the zero power is defined as equal to 1.

In the counting system we use today—the decimal positional notation system, to give it its full title—we use a base of 10. But there is absolutely no reason—except perhaps the number of fingers on a pair of human hands—that we do not instead write numbers with a base of 12 or 20. For over half the course of civilization the scientists of the Western world wrote their fractions by a positional notation system on a different base. This was a breathtakingly sophisticated "sexagesimal" system worked out by the ancient Mesopotamins on the number 60.

Although 60 is an extraordinarily large number to use as the base for a notation system, we still use it every day in our division of an hour into 60 minutes, of a minute into 60 seconds, and of a circle into six times 60^0. If a naval officer tells his men to synchronize their watches at 5:07:09, they know that he means nine seconds and seven minutes after 5 a.m. Few would be able to decipher the ancient 60-based number 5,7,9 (by which the Mesopotamians meant $5 \times 60^2 + 7 \times 60^1 + 9 \times 60^0$), but if they could they would arrive at the modern number 18,429. And that is what 5:07:09 means: exactly 18,429 seconds after midnight.

The 60-system had one important drawback born of its broad base. To represent each number from zero to 59, the Mesopotamians faced the prospect of devising 59 separate symbols. No one, not even the number-loving Sumerians and Babylonians who successively inhabited Mesopotamia, ever wanted to memorize 59 numerals any more than we today relish memorizing over 120 telephone area codes. To get around this difficulty, the ancients used combinations of two wedge-shaped symbols, one representing the number 1, the other representing the number 10.

With its one disadvantage, the 60-system also had certain virtues. The number 60 can be evenly divided by 1,2,3,4,5,6,10,12,15,20,30 and 60, whereas 10 can be evenly divided only by 1,2,5 and 10. This means that arithmetic problems worked out in the 60-system more frequently came out in even answers than they do in the 10-system. What was perhaps more important to the Mesopotamins, who were avid astronomers, the base of 60 fitted well with their division of a year into 360 days.

The 60-system came into being before 1700 B.C. Cuneiform tablets of this era show that by then it was already being used for amazing feats of computation by mathematicians of the reign of Babylon's intellectual King Hammurabi. But as yet they had no symbol for zero. To indicate an empty position in a number sequence, they left a gap. But since they often forgot to do so, the numbers were sometimes ambiguous.

By about 300B.C., the era of the next great group of cuneiform tablets which archeologists have unearthed, a symbol for zero had appeared—a mark somewhat resembling an upended W During this period the Persians ruled Mesopotamia, and the 60-system showed a considerable development beyond its original form. Mathematicians were carrying out their calculations to seventeen 60-system places, or what in our present notation would amount to 29-digit numbers. The prodigious nature of this achievement can be gauged by a look at a 60- system sequence of a mere four places. If, for instance, the Persians wished to express the number five million eleven thousand one hundred and sixty -seven, they did it as 23,11,59,27—which means $23 \times 60^3 + 11 \times 60^4 + 59 \times 60^9 + 27 \times 60^0$ (4,968,000 + 39,600+ 3,540 + 27=5,011,167).

The 60-system outlasted the mesopotamians who fathered it because its positional notation remained, for centuries, the only one extant. Greek astronomers and their Hindu counterparts in the early Christian era used it to record, in positional form, the fractions involved in charting the heavens. The Greeks and Hindus also utilized the 10-system, but only for simple counting, since at that stripling stage of its development the 10-system lacked a positional notation. The letters of the Greek and Hindu alphabets served as symbols for the decimal numbers

Then, probably around 500A.D., some Hindu devised a positional notation for the decimal system. The Hindus threw out the now-needless letter symbols they had used for numbers higher than 9 and standardized the symbols for the first nine. Although subsequently modernized, these nine Hindu letter symbols are what we today know as numbers 1 through 9. The all-important zero sign did not come along until the decimal positional notation had been further developed.

The first great popularizer of this notation was an Arab mathematician, al-Khowarizmi of Baghdad, who around 825 wrote a book on the Indian numerals in which he commended the new technique from the East to mathematicians and merchants everywhere. They were slow to heed his sage advice. It took the new numbers' about two centuries to reach Spain, where they were reconstituted in a recognizably modern script known as the Ghobar numerals —so called, it is thought, after the Arabic word for dust, or sand, which occasionally was used in a sort of computational sandbox. By the late 13th Century the city-state of Florence was passing laws against the use of the upstart decimal numerals to protect honest citizens from the easy changes which forgers of bank drafts, for instance, could ring on the number 0,6 and 9. About the same time the new number-writing technique arrived in England in a book called *Crafte of Nombrynge.*

The 10-based positional notation system ultimately won out over earlier systems because it was taken up by European merchants. Most likely the Araby-Indy experts in the counting houses of the larger shipping firms of Genoa and Hamburg found that they could do accounts faster than colleagues who specialized, say, in Roman numerals. The enthusiasm of the businessmen was not initially shared by the scientists and scholars, and for good reason. As yet the decimal system had no easy way to denote fractions. For this vital aspect of computation, learned circles continued to rely upon the ancient 60-system.

For our own convenient way of designating decimal fractions—Rs. 0.23 rupee for 23/100 of a rupee, or. 365 for a ballplayer's batting average—we can thank certain inventive thinkers of both Asia and Europe. One was al-Kashi 15th Century director of the astronomical observatory at Samarkand founded by Ulugh Beg, grandson of Tamerlane the Conqueror. Al-Kashi was among the first-known mathematicians to perceive that negative powers could be exploited in the 10-system as well as in the 60-system. A 16th Century German, Christoff Rudolff, produced a further clarifying explanation. Then a Belgian, Simon Stevin, presented the first systematic treatment of the new decimal fractions in a landmark opus entitled *La Disme (The Art of Tenths).* The decimal point as we know it made its debut in 1617 in a book by a Scotsman, John Napier.

Pure mathematics—for its own sake, without any practical goal in mind—began when man first thought of numbers as numbers, apart from the count of his sheep, and when he first thought of shapes as shapes, apart from the turn of a vase. But this early pure mathematics was not the logical, systematic kind that we know today. The forgotten geniuses of Mesopotamia who invented the 60-system seldom paused to ponder the connections between their discoveries or to delve deeply into the thought processes by which they arrived at them.

Prior to the Greeks, mathematicians did not expect anyone to be interested in the mental struggles they had gone through to reach a result—a formula, say, for the amount of stone needed to build a pyramid. If the result worked, that was proof enough of its validity. The Greeks were not merely content to show that a result worked. They wanted to explain why, and this they tried to do by the shortest, strictest logical argument they could devise. The writing of proofs became and art in which it was a matter of pride to be as economical as possible with the steps in reasoning and yet leave no loopholes. Greek mathematics accumulated a repertory of proved theorems, any one of which could be used without re-proof to formulate some more advanced theorem. Moreover, all the theorems could be arranged, tier upon tier, in an ever widening inverted pyramid of knowledge. The point at the bottom of the pyramid could be firmly embedded in everyday experience through a few self-evident axioms, such as *the shortest distance between two points is a straight line or two straight lines can cross only once.*

As mathematics progressed, the so-called level of rigor—the measure of what constitutes an acceptable formal proof—kept rising, like a water level. As a result, modern mathematicians have found hidden assumptions in some of the Greek proofs. They have even turned up a few limitations in the axiomatic method itself. They have had to devise other sets of axioms on which to construct the newer branches of mathematics. But the basic Greek system of abstraction and proof remains intact. Every branch of modern mathematics, insofar as possible, is organized according to this system.

The springboard for the Greeks' epochal revolution in thought was geometry, With their natural artistic bent, they were instinctively drawn to the neatness and visual appeal of this mathematics of points, lines, areas and volumes. Both the Babylonians and Egyptians had employed a rough-and-ready geometry in land-surveying and building measurements, but simply as practical applications of counting —in terms, for instance, of the number of tile facings or solid stone blocks required for the west wall of the new palace. The Greeks had a far more abstract approach. They believed that a shape of a certain kind has innate unchanging properties which are independent of its size. Thus, a 45° right triangle—one that has tow equal sides—may extend all the way to the moon or it may lie on the head of a pin, but in either case it remains a 45° right triangle.

The first Greek to grasp this fundamental possibility for abstraction in geometry—and to glimpse the Greek dream that knowledge would rise in solid inverted pyramids of proof from a few elementary axioms—was probably Thales of Miletus, an enterprising olive-oil tycoon who operated along the coasts of Asia Minor from about 600 to 550B.C. In his travels he had come in contact with the lore of the old mathematics and astronomy, and in his retirement he took them up as a hobby, The five propositions which he is credited with demonstrating—seen in the margins below—were so simple as to indicate that he was consciously trying to establish the foundation of geometry in unshakably basic terms.

Thales' ambition might have remained unfulfilled had it not been for another Greek who, it is believed, studied with him. This was Pythagoras, a man of magnetic and forceful personality. Legend has it that at Thales' recommendation Pythagoras spent years in travel, seeking to enlarge his mathematical understanding. Among the sources he is said to have tapped were the priests of Zoroaster—the wise men, or Magi, of the Christmas story—who had become custodian of Mesopotamian mathematical lore under the Persian Empire. Then, having learned all he could, Pythagoras about 540 B.C. founded a semi-religious, semi-mathematical cult in Crotona, a burgeoning Greek colonial town on the instep of the Italian boot. Along with mathematics, he taught his disciples to worship numbers; to believe in reincarnation and the transmigration of souls from man to man and man to beast; never to eat beans; always to remain anonymous and sign the neme of the Pythagorean brotherhood to any writing or discovery.

The best-remembered of the Pythagorean teachings, is of course, the theorem that in a right triangle the square on the long side—the hypotenuse—is equal to the sum of the squares on the two shorter sides. The Babylonians had discovered this theorem a millennium earlier, but the Pythagorean school is credited as the first to prove it. It is still tremendously useful in science. But what is of more down-to-earth interest for most of us, carpenters depend on the principle behind the theorem to make sure that the rooms they lay out are perfect rectangles.

Pythagoras made a second highly practical contribution, which figures in every performance by a jazz pianist or string quartet. This was his discovery of the underlying mathematics of the musical scale. Pythagoras found that a marvelous connection existed between musical harmony and the whole numbers we count by —1, 2, 3, 4, 5 and so. Pluck a string and sound a note, then pluck and equally taut string twice as long and you hear a new note just one harmonic octave below the first. starting with any string and the note is sounds, you can go down the scale by increasing the length of the string according to simple fractions expressible as the ratios of whole numbers. For instance, 16/15 of a C-string gives the next lower note B, 6/5 of it gives A, 4/3 of it gives G, 3/2 of its gives F. 8/5 of it gives E, 16/9 of it gives D, and exactly two of it give C again, an octave lower. Pythagoras discovered the whole-number relationships between C, F, G and low C and between their equivalents in any scale. From this find he progressed to the firms conviction that all harmony, all beauty, all nature can be expressed by whole-number relationships. He even believed that the planets, as they move in their orbits, must give off a heavenly whole-numbered harmony—the so-called "music of the spheres.".

So enraptured were the Pythagoreans by the peerless power of the integers, so certain were they that the entire universe was made up of these whole numbers, that they took to classifying them into categories such as "perfect" and "amicable." They also labeled the even numbers as feminine and the old numbers as masculine —excepting only the number 1, which they regarded as the generator of all the numbers. Then, in the wake of this charming fantasy, a sobering discovery was made, one so un-Pythagorean that the brotherhood tried to suppress it.

The disturbing find was a new kind of number—one which we today call and irrational. The characteristic of the irrational is that is remains stubbornly unwhole no matter what. This maddening trait turns up frequently in what we call a square root—the quantity which, when multiplied by itself, produces the given number. The square root of 4 (symbolically written as $\sqrt{4}$) is neat, tidy 2; $\sqrt{9}$ is 3. but an irrational square root turns out to be a decimal fraction with an endless series of non-repeating digits after the decimal point. For example, $\sqrt{2}$ is 1.41421.....and so on *ad infinitum*, $\sqrt{3}$ is 1.73205...... *ad infinitum*. Even more unsettling to the orderly mind, irrational square roots crop up with dismaying frequency.

The case of the right triangle will serve as an example. A right triangle whose short sides are three and Tour units long and whose whole hypotenuse is an even five units long is very exceptional. For every one of its kind—every 3-4-5, 5-12-13 or 7-24-25 triangle— there are innumerable "imperfect" right triangles with sides like 1-1-$\sqrt{2}$ or 1-2-$\sqrt{5}$ or 2-$\sqrt{5}$-3. Suppose you are measuring a field laid out in the form of right triangle with two equal sides and a third long side. Suppose the two equal sides come out evenly in feet. Then the third side will not come out evenly—no matter if you measure it in microcaliper fractions of an inch or centimeter—or if you start all over again to measure in cubits or furlongs. No matter how many times you subdivide the length of the long side, you will never come out with a subdivision that equals a subdivision of the length of either short side. Between the long and either of the short sides there is no common measure whatsoever.

The Pythagoreans realized that in most right triangles the irreducible ratios between the lengths of the sides could not be expressed in terms of whole numbers, not even if all the whole numbers and all their fractions—from 1 to a trillion of from 1/1 to a trillionth—were called into service for the attempt. This crushing discovery affected the entire course of Greek mathematical thinking. It effectively dashed any hope that measurement might be used as a bridge between geometry and the arithmetic of whole numbers. The Greeks began to restrict themselves to shape-geometry, which concerned itself not with measurement but only with shape. The could thus draw, if not measure, certain irrational numbers such as $\sqrt{2}$ or $\sqrt{3}$, as a definite hypotenuse in a definite right triangle. Just like rambunctious children, these could at least be corralled within definitely bordered rectilinear figures—triangles, squares and pyramids.

But neither irrationals nor the concept of infinity would stay out of even the most elementary shape-geometry. After triangles, both cropped up again in the problem of the circle. The ratio of a circle's circumference to its diameter is itself an irrational number, 3.14159......, which we call pi, or symbolically π. (It is believed that the first letter of the Greek word *periphereia*—meaning "periphery"—inspired the π symbol. Whatever its origin, the quantity it represents has been calculated it more than 100,000 decimal places, and we know that it will never come out evenly.) The Greeks did not recognize the full extent of π's irrationality, and so they wasted much labor trying to solve the one big problem which this fact made impossible—constructing a square 'whole area is equal to that of a given circle, or literally trying to "square the circle."

The best way they could assess the area of a circle itself was as the sum of an infinite number of infinitely narrow triangles ranged around the center of the circle like so many stingy silvers of apple pie. The height of each infinitely narrow triangle was the same as the radius of the circle. The sum of the infinitely short bases of all the triangles was the same as the circumference of the circle. And since the combined area of all the triangles should equal half their height times the sum of their bases, the area of the circle should equal half its radius times its circumference. There was nothing wrong with this conclusion. It worked. But trying to prove it by rigorous step-by-step logic was an intellectual journey as arduous as the odyssey of Ulysses. As a triangle becomes infinitely narrow, exactly when does it cease to be ◄-shaped and start to behave as if it were a ◄-shaped silver of pie? Surely it does not take on the shape of a proper pie-slice until it is infinitely narrow and then, surely, it is no longer something but nothing. How can an infinite number of nothings be added up to produce a something such as a circle?

These troublesome objections to the logic of fine-slicing a circle were posed—probably with glee—by the Eleatic school of philosophers, a school which had come into being at Elea, next door to Crotona and the Pythagoreans. From the start the Eleatics seem to have opposed the Pythagoreans. Mathematics was no mere pastime for the Greeks; its problems were fought out in an open arena. What in retrospect seems a serene and unimpeded parade of progress toward greater knowledge was, in fact, an intellectual war waged with all the fervor of a wine shop controversy. The weapons of this war were sophisticated arguments. Its ultimate prize was the triumph of proof.

The Eleatics were deeply interested in scientific understanding—not just of triangles and circles but of the whole cosmos. Their leading spokesman was Zeno, master of that perplexing device, the paradox—a proposition which, though valid logically, flies in the face of common sense. Zeno was fascinated by the idea of infinity. He rightly felt that science could not grapple with reality unless it took into account the ways infinity seems to appear everywhere in nature. He posed a simple question involving motion and propounded a new-celebrated paradox. How is it possible for a moving point to pass through an infinite number of positions in a finite time? If the fleet-footed Achilles runs a race with a tortoise and the tortoise is given as much as a foot's (30-cm) head start, how can Achilles—by rigorous Greek logic—ever catch up? When Achilles has gone a foot, the tortoise has also trudged ahead by, say, a tenth of a foot. And when Achilles has covered the tenth, the tortoise is still some farther distance on its way.

Anyone knows from experience that Achilles can catch up with the tortoise, but how does anyone prove it by logical steps that do not need an infinity of pages for the proving? Modem mathematicians have ways of sidestepping the problem and so did the Greeks. One of the early sages of geometry, probably Eudoxus, supplemented the controversial proof about the area of a circle with two subsidiary lines of reasoning. These showed that if the area of a circle is more or less than half its circumference times its radius, contradictions arise—contradictions which reduce the altemnatives to absurdities (thus, again, *reductio ad absurdum*).

At about the same time that Eudoxus was scoring this point over the Eleatics and infinity, the old Greek world was being swallowed up in the almost infinite conquests of Alexander the Great. When the clangor of arms had subsided, a new capital of Greek culture emerged at Alexandria in Egypt. And there, about 300 B.C., the most famous of all masters of geometry, Euclid, set out to collect the theorems of his predecessors and to arrange them as a single self-contained whole.

Euclid was not himself a great innovator, but he was a superb organizer of the mathematical results achieved by Thales, Eudoxus and other luminaries of the golden age of Greek geometry—men who are no more than names to us now, such as Democritus, Hippocrates of Chios, and Archytas. Euclid was eminently skilled at rewriting their proofs in terse, clear terms. Thus simplified, they are contained in his master-piece, the *Elements*, one of those unique books like the Bible which seem to fuse the best efforts of generations of creative minds into a single inspired whole.

After Euclid, mathematicians could only go up—out of the realms normally thought of as Greek geometry into the rarefied atmosphere of what is popularly known as higher mathematics. Inspired by the *Elements*, the two most gifted mathematicians of the next century were to originate as many new results and generate as many useful formulas as all the pre-Euclidean Greeks put together. One was Apollonius, whose discoveries about the so-called conic sections later contributed importantly to astronomy, to the military science of ballistics and finally to modern rocketry. The other was Archimedes, whose brilliance at mathematics was matched by a genius for mechanics which made him the father of practical engineering.

So far as possible, both Apollonius and Archimedes conducted their higher mathematical researches within the rigorous discipline imposed on geometry by the renowned Athenian philosopher Plato. Because he thought in terms of the pure ideal, the totally abstract, Plato was devoted to geometry; he liked the way it could abstract from a bumpy cart wheel to the concept of a circle immune from time and change. Because of his prestige, he was able to communicate his enthusiasm to his fellow citizens, thereby giving the practitioners of geometry a high place in public esteem. But while conferring this cachet upon them, he also saddled them with a difficult work restriction. Frowning, philosopher-like, upon mere mechanical discovery and applied mathematics, Plato insisted that geometric proofs be demonstrated with no aids other than a straight-edge and a compass. This requirement, which did not originate with Plato but took stimulus from him, applied across the board to all elementary geometric problems and when feasible to advanced problems.

Appollonius made his contribution to mathematical history by investigating all the most important quirks of a series of graceful curves which he described in a book entitled *Conics*. He called them conics because he visualized them as cuts made by a flat or plane surface when it intersects the surface of a cone; it was as if he mentally took a hack saw to an ice cream cone. Depending on how the cone was cut, the resulting dissections were circles, ellipses, parabolas or hyperbolas. Then he investigated the properties of each conic cut and showed how they are all interrelated. As pure mathematics all these ingenious labors need no justification, but they have turned out to be doubly justified by the fact that conic sections are the paths which projectiles, satellites, moons or earths follow under in influence of gravity around planets or stars.

Apollonius' rival and friend was Archimedes, who was a little more brilliant and a great deal more creative—so much so that within the profession he is ranked, with Newton and Gauss, as one of the three great mathematicians of all time. Everything that Archimedes did seems as modern in spirit today as when he created it. Yet he created all that he did within the extremely narrow bounds of Platonic discipline, without any form of algebraic shorthand to catalyze his logic and without even a convenient system of notation for writing large numbers and doing complicated arithmetic.

Most Greeks had no simple way of writing really large numbers. Archimedes faced up to this severe disadvantage in a scientific treatise, the *Sand Reckoner*, setting forth a system of numbers based on the Greek myriad, or 10,000. Numbers up to a myriad of myriads, or 100 million, he called "the first order of numbers." Numbers up to a myriad of myriads multiplied by themselves a myriad myriad times—$100{,}000{,}000^{100{,}000{,}000}$—he called "numbers of the first period." He went on to let this enormous number be multiplied by itself a myriad myriad times, arriving at a quantity so vast that in 10-system notation it would be written as a 1 followed by 80 million billion zeros. This impressive cavalcade, he pointed out, is a quite adequate number.

The achievement of which Archimedes himself was most proud was the discovery of how to calculate the volume of a sphere. He found that the volume of a sphere equals two thirds the volume of the smallest possible cylinder which will enclose it. To show that a cylinder is half again as voluminous as its "inscribed sphere," Archimedes had to apply the same technique of infinite fine-slicing that earlier Greeks had used on the area of a circle, Then he had to prove by the method of *reductio ad absurdum* that if more or less than two thirds of the circumscribing cylinder equaled the volume of the sphere, the results would lead to contradiction. He employed the same technique to demonstrate what areas were enclosed within parabolic curves and certain spiral curves. He used it again to compute the volume of space which a conic section sweeps out as it rotates on its axis.

Because of his practical turn of mind, Archimedes was a physicist and engineer as well as a mathematician. Many who know little else about him remember him as a sort of absent-minded professor who ran naked through the streets of the Sicilian city of Syracuse, where he lived, crying, "Eureka, Eureka!"—meaning "I have found it!" What he had actually found was a physicist's fact, a basic law of hydraulic engineering. Any bath-taker is aware that a solid sunk in a liquid displaces its own *volume* of that liquid. But Archimedes discovered that a solid floating on a liquid displaces its own *weight* of that liquid and in general that a solid immersed in a liquid loses exactly as much weight as the weight of the liquid it pushed aside.

"Aha, its whole, its seventh, it makes 19." Strange-sounding patter this, suggestive of some occult ritual, but we echo it oftener than we realize. This brief sentence, discovered in a 3,600-year-old Egyptian papyrus, poses one of the first algebra problems known to have been solved by man. The explosive-sounding "Aha" is intended not as an exclamation but simply to designate "a heap," or "quantity." We use its equivalent every time we say : "Let χ equal......."

The papyrus of "Aha" came to the notice of Western scholars a century ago. Henry Rhind, a tuberculosis-ridden Scottish antiquary, bought it in 1858 in a shop in the Nile village of Luxor, where he was wintering for his health. Called the Rhind Papyrus in his honor, it is one of the earliest mathematical documents extant—

an especially interesting one because of the evidence it contains that men in 1700 B.C. were already dealing with the kinds of problems we now solve with algebra. From the days of the Pharaohs on down, men have sought the same mathematical goal : to permit the solution of a mathematical problem which involves an unknown number. In modern algebra the unknown is expressed by an abstract symbol that is manipulated until its numerical value can be established. In order to pin the problem down while it is being turned around and simplified, the relationship between known and unknown numbers is set down in an equation—a statement of what equals what.

The venerable Egyptian problem of "Aha, its whole, its seventh, it makes 19" can readily be transmuted into 20th Century terms. A hard-pressed taxpayer faces the prospect of filing a declaration of estimated income tax. He knows that his actual tax will be Rs. 1,900. But he decides that if he slightly underestimates it at the beginning of the year—so that the balance he will have to make up at the end of the year does not exceed one seventh of what he has estimated—the Internal Revenue Service will not make a federal case out of it. Using the marvelously timesaving shorthand and rule book logic of modern algebra, he says to himself : "Let x equal the number of hundreds of dollars I will declare as my tax. Then the problem is to find χ so that χ plus one seventh of it will equal 19." He expresses the entire problem as an equation $\chi + \chi/7 = 19$ ("one seventh of χ" being $\chi/7$). Then, almost automatically, he follows the axiom that equals multiplied by equals remain equal, and he multiplies both sides of the equation by 7 to arrive at a new equation, $7\chi + \chi = 133$. This in turn gives him $8\chi = 133$, then $\chi = 133/8$, and, finally, $\chi = 16\frac{5}{8}$, or, in another form, $16\frac{5}{8}$ hundreds of rupees—an estimated tax of Rs. 1,662.50. The ancient Egyptians also reached the answer of $16\frac{5}{8}$, although without the symbolic sort of equation we use today.

Many a citizen goes happily through life without ever needing to solve an algebraic equation from the time he leaves school. But in the vastly complicated world beyond his door, such equations are indispensable for reducing tough problems to simple terms. A corporation wrestles with an equation when it decides how long to keep a machine that depreciates at so many dollars per year before replacing it with a new piece of equipment that costs such-and-such. Algebra is used to determine how a timer should be set so that a bomb dropped from 10,000 feet (3,048m), say, will explode 500 feet (152m) above the target. Few scientists can even talk without algebraic symbols to augment what they are saying. On office blackboards, cafeteria napkins or the hot sands of beaches, they are constantly scribbling equations—as terse summaries of past experiments or as handles with which to grasp at the possibilities of nature.

Modern algebra's procedures are as clear-cut as the regulations in an army manual. Write the problem as an equation in terms of χ, the unknown number. Systematically arrange all the terms involving χ on one side of the equation. Then combine and reduce them by symbolic arithmetic until a single χ is left on one side and a known number on the other. This is the answer. Although simple-sounding in theory, in practice the transformations which have to be wrought to reduce the various terms involving χ to a single χ can be intricate and laborious. Sometimes it is helpful to break a problem down into several sub-problems. Sometimes it is helpful to substitute for a combination of χ's a single new unknown—a *y* or a *z*—which can be carried along like a traveler's check and then converted back into the hard cash of χ at journey's end.

Algebra's major difficulties arise because some problems involve not just χ, but also χ^2 or χ^3. The easy equations involving only χ—and no higher power of χ—are called first-degree, or linear, equations ("linear" meaning "one-dimenstional"). Second-degree equations—containing no powers higher than χ^2—are called quadratics (from "quadrate," or "squared number"). Equations of the third degree are called cubics; of the fourth degree, quartics. Beyond the quartics are indefinitely many equations of the fifth, sixth or umpteenth degree. Fortunately, these fearsome high-degree equations come up only occasionally.

Most everyday problems in algebra—how fast to drive χ miles to get to an appointment on time, how to convert a recipe for four into dinner for five—can be posed as linear equations. Quadratics come up mainly in two-dimenstional problems, such as those involving area—how wide a sidewalk may be built around a rectangular lot of a certain size with a certain amount of cement. Cubics arise in three-dimensional problems, such as those concerning volume—how much metal is needed to build a million-gallon (3,785 kl) spherical oil tank. Quartics and higher-degree equations are required for complex questions, such as finding the constant reproduction rate at which a bacterium will spawn a given number of descendants in *n* generations—a so-called *n*th-degree equation. (Contrary to popular impression, the "*n*th degree" is not the ultimate degree" to mathematicians but just any unspecified degree)

To make matters easier all around, all equations of a given degree are viewed as a family. And just as each Scottish Highland clan has its own tartan, so each family of equations has its own representative "general equation." In this, a letter from the end of the alphabet —χ, *y* or *z*— represents the unknown number, while letters from the beginning of the alphabet —*a*, *b*, *c*— represent numbers assumed to be known but not yet specified. Every quadratic equation, for instance, can be represented by the single general equation $a\chi^2+b\chi+c=0$. By solving this purely symbolic relationship, algebraists have found that the solution χ is always

$$\frac{-b \pm \sqrt{b^2 - 4ac}}{2a}$$

In this formula, familiar to all students of high-school algebra, the ±(plus-or-minus) sign means that there are two solutions to every quadratic equation—one which can be found by adding, the other by subtracting, at that particular point in the calculation.

No surprisingly, the general solutions of the cubic and quartic families are correspondingly more complicated. As for the upper-crust equations beyond the quartic, no general solutions have been worked out at all. In fact, mathematicians have proved that equations beyond the fourth degree cannot be solved, by algebraic methods, in their full generality. With the help of the trial-and-error technique of an electronic computer, they can work out the solution for any specific problem involving a high-degree equation—but they cannot write down an exact algebraic formula for this solution.

Solving equations in algebra is greatly simplified by the signs and symbols that are employed; they serve as a shorthand to set in sharp relief both the problems and the logical steps for finding solutions. Astonishingly, in view of algebra's antiquity, the advantage of symbols went long unrealized. It was the 17th Century French philosopher-mathematician Rene Descartes who first used *a*, *b* and *c* to represent the known numbers and who, with a Gallic flair for the logical, decided that the other end of the alphabet should provide the symbols for the unknown. It was Descartes, too, who began to write χ^2 in place of $\chi\chi$ or χ^5 for $\chi\chi\chi\chi\chi$. From then on algebraic equations could be written in substantially their modern form.

Before an algebraic notation was developed, and before the birth of the idea that equations could be classified and that each class of equations had a general solution, algebra problems had the same dark fascination that riddles have. Each was a separate case with its own special solution. To the ancient mathematician, exploring his new-found land, each problem was an unexpected palace standing alone in a trackless wilderness. Today, looking at the terse records of early algebraic discoverers, we have no way of knowing what paths they took to their palaces and why. The first scholars who fully explained their methods for solving algebra problems—linear, quadratic and cubic—were the incomparable Greeks. But they wrote out their solutions in words and diagrams only—a long process and sometimes a confusing one.

Then, in the twilight of the Greek era, a singular man appeared—Diophantus, who has been called the "Father of Algebra." Of his dates, we know only that they fell sometime between 100 and 400 A.D. By an odd happenstance, however, we do know precisely how long he lived—84 years. We have this information because one of his admirers described his life in terms of an algebraic riddle (shown below). Since the equation used to solve this riddle is an easy linear one, without any χ^2 or χ^3 in it, Diophantus himself would probably have turned up his nose at it. He was intent on tougher equations of other types.

Diophantus is remembered as the father of algebra because he was the first to abbreviate his thoughts systematically with symbols of his own devising and because he solved what are now called indeterminate, or "Diophantine," equations. Indeterminate equations do not contain enough information to be solved in specific numbers but enough to tie the answer down to a definite type. For instance : Mary is a year more than 10 times as old as Joan. What is Mary's age ? Evidently, if Joan is 1,2,3,4.....100......years old, Mary is 11, 21, 31, 41.......1,001.......years old. The equation connecting their ages, $\chi = 10y+1$, seems a trivial one at first sight, but it conjures up two entire parades of whole numbers marching in $x=10y+1$ step all the way to infinity. By using such infinite trains of numbers, correlated through Diophantine equations, modern mathematicians can study the properties of various types of whole numbers such as odds, evens, primes or squares, and can grasp some of the basic rules which numbers follow in playing the tricks they do.

The analysis of numbers that has grown from Diophantine equations is called the "theory of numbers" and is the purest of pure branches of present mathematics. Its development by Diophantus helped algebraists to look on an equation as a way of categorizing all numbers of a given type rather than as a relationship solely between the numbers of a specific problem. Algebra slowly began to unfold as a separate discipline.

During the Dark and Middle Ages a succession of Hindu and Moslem mathematicians handed algebra down from one oasis of culture—one sultanate or caliphate—to the next. They did not create much new knowledge in the process, but at least through practice they stripped the art of a equations of its aura of mystery. In 825 A.D. *al-Khowarizmi*, the same sage of Baghdad who had publicized the positional 10-system of writing numbers, wrote the first clear textbook on algebra. The title of this influential work was *al-jabr w'al-muqabalah*, which, translated from the Arabic, roughly means "the art of bringing together unknowns to match a known quantity." They key word in the title, *al-jabr*, or "bringing together," gave rise to our word algebra. Curiously, in medieval times "algebraist" could refer either to a man who brought bones together, *i.e.* a surgeon or to a specialist in equations.

The most significant problem left hanging by al-Khowarizmi and his predecessors was how to interpret negative numbers—the numbers less than zero. After all, what could a negative number mean? Who ever held in his hand less than nothing? Today every beginning student in algebra learns by rote the so-called "law of signs"—that a plus times a plus equals a plus, that a minus times a minus equals a plus and that a plus times a minus equals a minus. The Hindus, it is believed, were among the first to perceive the possibilities of these combinations, and to realize that in solving a quadratic equation one can come up with a negative for an answer. Because 2×2 and -2×-2 both equal 4, for instance, the equation $x^2 = 4$ has not only the obvious solution $x = +2$ but also the solution

$x = -2$.

Since it is hard to grasp the idea of negative numbers, a long time elapsed before they were allowed into the parlors of mathematical propriety and common sense. One of the first to give them open-minded consideration was an Italian mathematician, Leonardo da Pisa, otherwise called "Fibonacci," who lived from about 1170 to 1250 A.D. On one occasion, while tackling a financial problem, he saw that it just could not be solved except in terms of a negative number. Instead of shrugging off this number, he looked it squarely in the eye and described it as a financial loss. "This problem," he wrote, "I have shown to be insoluble unless it is conceded that the first man had a debt."

Negative numbers can, of course, be interpreted in many other ways. They measure distances back along a road, temperatures below zero, times before the present or minutes before the hour. In general they are numbers with an arrow of direction built into them—an arrow that points backward from zero while the positive numbers point forward. As far as modern mathematicians are concerned, negative numbers need not be interpreted at all; they are simply useful abstractions.

Despite Fibonacci's tentative recognition that an equation might have a negative solution, most mathematicians continued to view negative numbers with cool disbelief until the 16th Century. In this, the era of the Renaissance, when explorers in all fields were daily proving that they could go beyond the ancients and find new things under the sun, mathematics too enjoyed a new burst of creativity. Man's conception of numbers began to enlarge beyond the names and digits with which he could count pebbles on a beach. He began to see numbers as creations of his own mind; they were figments, perhaps, but figments which would some day enable him to envision atomic particles and to label points in space and time. This insight emerged in connection with the investigation of the cubic, or third-degree, equation, which happened to represent the outstanding mathematical problem of the time.

By the 16th Century, general solutions had been found for the linear and quadratic equations but not for the cubic—a rather infrequent equation involving x^3. But by 1550 the conquest of the cubic had been achieved by several independent approaches. And in applying these general formulas to particular equations, their discoverers could not help observing, with considerable unease, that the numbers involved in the procedure were not always the familiar positive ones.

The first man to take up Pacioli's cubic challenge was Scipione del Ferro, a papermaker's son who had risen to become professor of mathematics at the University of Bologna. Finding the first general solution for all cubic equations of the simplified form $\chi^3 + a\chi = b$. del Ferro kept his discovery a secret, possibly to confound adversaries during competitions. But in his later years he confided his solution to his student Antonio Fior, who used it in an algebra match with a rival, Nicolo Fontana, called Tartaglia, or the "Stammerer," because as a boy he had had his palate cleft by a French saber.

By the time of the contest with Fior, Tartaglia had become one of the canniest equation-solvers in Italy and had devised a secret weapon of his own : a general solution for cubics of the type $\chi^3 + a\chi^2=b$. As a result, when Fior tossed him a group of specific examples of the $\chi^3 + a\chi = b$ type, he countered with examples of the $\chi^3 + a\chi^2 = b$ type. During the interval allowed for working out the answers, both Tartaglia and Fior worked feverishly, but when time was up and the day of reckoning had arrived, Tartaglia had solved all Fior's problems and Fior had solved none of Tartaglia's. The Stammerer's genius had responded to pressure by conceiving a general solution for *both* types of cubic equations.

Cardano formally accepted the concept of negative numbers and enunciated the laws which govern them. He also advanced yet another kind of new number which he called a "fictitious" or "sophistic" quantity. This was the square root of a negative number and even harder to grasp than a negative number itself, since no real number multiplied by itself can produce a negative number. Today mathematicians call the square root of a negative number, such as $\sqrt{-2}$, an "imaginary" number. When such a quantity is combined with a real number, such as in $1 + \sqrt{-2}$, the result is known as a "complex" number.

Later mathematicians have shown that complex numbers can have all sorts of applications : They provide solutions to equations concerning, for instance, the "states" of atomic particles in atomic physics. Like many concepts of mathematics, they are best accepted as pure abstractions. Cardano's premonition as to their importance, however, was more than justified when the 19th Century mathematical genius Carl Friedrich Gauss proved that every equation has exactly as many positive, negative or complex solutions as the degree of the equation itself. Every first degree equation has one solution, every second-degrees equation has two solutions, every third-degree equation has three solutions, every nth-degree equation has n solutions. This satisfying symmetry is called the "fundamental theorem of algebra."

Rene Descartes, a French, developed new branches of mathematics. This was "analytic geometry," which merged all the arithmetic, algebra and geometry of ages past in a single technique—a technique of visualizing numbers as points on a graph, equations as geometric shapes, and shapes as equations. By unifying elementary mathematics, analytic geometry became the bedrock on which was built most of today's higher mathematics and much of the exact sciences.

Descartes set forth the idea that a pair of numbers can determine a position on a surface : one number as a distance measured horizontally, the other as a distance measured vertically. This idea, of course, has since become familiar to anyone who has used graph paper, read a street map, or studied latitude and longitude lines in an atlas. Graph paper had not yet been invented in Descartes' day, but the concept of the graph itself, with its use of crossed lines for reference purposes, was contained in his work. Descartes showed that with a pair of intersecting straight lines as yardsticks, a whole net work of reference lines could be constructed on which numbers could be designated as points; that if algebraic equations were represented as sequences of points, they would appear as geometric shapes; and that geometric shapes, in turn, could be translated into sequences of numbers represented as sequences of points, they would appear as geometric shapes; and that geometric shapes, in turn, could be translated into sequences of numbers represented as equations. In Descartes' honor we call the original intersecting straight lines the system of "Cartesian coordinates," with the vertical line known as the y axis, the horizontal line as the χ axis.

In the concept of coordinates with which he launched his analytic geometry, Descartes gave all mathematicians of then and thereafter a stimulating new way to look at mathematical information. He showed, for instance, that all second-power, or quadratic, equations, when graphed as connected points, become straight lines, circles, ellipses, parabolas or hyperbolas—the conic sections on which Appollonius had lavished so much ingenuity 1,900 years earlier. The equation $\chi^2 - y^2 = 0$, when graphed' becomes two straight crossed lines, the equation $\chi^2 + y^2 = 4$ becomes a circle, $\chi^2 - y^2 = 4$ a hyperbola, $\chi^2 + 2y^2 = 4$ an ellipse, and $\chi^2 = 4y$ a parabola (illustrated at right). What is more, Descartes went on to show that the general equation representing all quadratics, $a\chi^2 + b\chi y + cy^2 = d$, inevitably turns into a conic curve when graphed.

Going beyond the quadratic to cubics, quartics and equations of even higher degree, Descartes established that each class of equations brings into being a whole new tribe of curves—hearts, hummocks, petal shapes, loops, figure eights. The degree of an equation determines the maximum number of intersection points that the curve of the equation can have with a straight line. A first-degree curve—that is, straight line—can intersect another straight line at only two points. Cubic curves, which a straight line can intersect three times, are often S-shaped. Fourth-degree curves, with four possible intersection points, may have the shape of a W or a figure 8. Even the hourglass of the feminine figure, some scholars have concluded, perhaps in their idle time, can be translated algebraically into a specific equation.

The curves which represent any one degree of equation have many other traits in common—so many, in fact, that each is a class unto itself, and a mathematician can say "fifth-degree" or "seventh-degree" curve to a colleague and conjure up a large array of specific geometric features peculiar to all members of the particular curvaceous tribe in question.

Thanks to analytic geometry, every equation can be converted into a geometric shape and every geometric shape into an equation. Some shapes, to be sure, can be represented only by indefinitely long equations and some equations represent shapes hard to visualize—full of dips and doubling-backs. But every shape has its equivalent in algebraic form.

In its all-encompassing embrace of past mathematical knowledge, analytic geometry was to grow far beyond Descartes' original brief presentation, and was to touch nothing in mathematics without transforming it, Branches of mathematical thought which had seemed sidelines were now brought into the mainstream. One was the ancient technique of trigonometry; another was the fledgling device of logarithms.

Trigonometry—the study of triangles—had served, from early Babylon until just prior to Descartes, as a purely practical adjunct of surveying, astronomy and navigation. Stargazers and sailors alike, scanning the heavens or the seas, often needed to calculate distances immeasurable by ruler or tape. Trigonometry permitted them to do so by simply applying certain basic rules about the relationships between the sides and angles of any triangle, however large or small. These relationships, or ratios, were initially established by the Greeks to analyze the areas of circles. To first man known to have employed such relationships was the astronomer Hipparchus, who used them around 140 B.C. to find straight-line distances across the curved vault of the heavens—an attempt, as it were, to eliminate the pi in the sky. Today the three most-used ratios concern the right triangle, and are called the sine (sin for short), the cosine (cos) and the tangent (tan). Precisely what these ratios represent, and how the homeowner applies them to fell a tree outside his house without smashing the roof.

The ratios represented by the sine, cosine and tangent of an angle change in numerical value as the angle changes in size. The Greeks calculated some of these values and arranged them in trigonometric tables which later mathematicians improved and extended. These tables remained, for a long time, merely a form of applied mathematics—the tool of celestial and earthly navigators. Then the remarkable French algebraist Francis Vieta, who preceded Descartes by half a century, made a vital observation. He perceived that a trigonometric ratio could be used to solve an algebraic equation; that, in effect, a series of numbers in a table could represent the successive values taken on by an unknown. The statement that "the sine of angle *x* is *y*" can also be put as "$y=\sin x$," an equation every bit as valid, say, as $y=x^2+7x$. The way Vieta's insight broadened the scope of trigonometry became even clearer when Descartes came along with his graphing technique. An equation like $y=\sin x$ could now be actually graphed, point by point, to create a curve on paper; it is, incidentally, an endless wavy line—the exact graphic equivalent of the pulsating ebb and flow of electric current in an ordinary A.C. power cable.

As it did with trigonometry, the Cartesian system reached out and took in the sideline of mathematics known to every teenager as "logarithms." Like trigonometry, logarithms involve relationships between numbers. A logarithm is the "exponent" of a number, indicating to what power the number must be raised in order to produce another given number. By familiarizing himself with logarithms, anyone confronted with arduous multiplications and divisions can save himself a lot of sheer arithmetic drudgery. This was precisely the intent of the inventor of arithmetic drudgery. This was precisely the intent of the inventor of logarithms, John Napier, Baron of Merchiston, the same man who first used the decimal point in its modern context.

This modest Scotsman conceived the idea of logarithms four decades before Descartes published his *Method.* The essence of Napier's discovery, as developed by later mathematicians, is that any number, of any size, can be expressed in terms of the power to which another number, the "base," must be raised to give the original number. For example, 100 is 10^2, 56 is $10^{1.74819}$ and 23 is $10^{1.36173}$. Further, when exponents of these last two 10s are added together, the result is a new power of 10, $10^{3.10992}$, which, when worked out, is 1,288, or 56 multiplied by 23. Subtracting the smaller of these same two exponents from the larger yields $10^{0.38646}$, which, when worked out, is the number that results from dividing 56 by 23, 2.4348. Mathematicians have enunciated all this in the so-called "laws of exponents" : Adding exponents is equivalent to multiplication, subtracting them is equivalent to division.

Napier arranged his logarithmic calculations in convenient tables, similar to the ones used by scientists and engineers for their multi digit calculations. To figure out 56,times 23, of course, should require no more than pencil and scratch paper or, at most, the handy aid to short calculation known as a slide rule—a gadget consisting of a pair of rulers marked off in logarithmic scales and fastened together so they can slide on one another. Where Napier's noble handiwork shows up best is in the wearisome longer computations—when, for instance, an economist decides to divide $503,443,000,000, the U.S. gross national product for 1960, by the U.S. population for that year, 179,323,175.

The development of the Cartesian system made it possible to draw curves for logarithmic relationships like $y=\log \chi$ as easily as it did for trigonometric ratios like $y = \sin \chi$. By permitting such equations, as well as all algebraic equations, to be displayed in visible, viable lines and points, the Cartesian graph in effect captured and tamed the changing relationships between interconnected quantities. Out of this triumph emerged a concept fundamental to all higher mathematics : the idea of "variables" and "functions."

If an χ and a y can be related through an equation or graph, they are called "variables". That is, one changes in value as the other changes in value. The two have what is known as a functional relationship; the variable whose change of value comes about as a result of the other variable's change of value is called a "function" of that other variable. A sine or a cosine or a tangent of an angle is a function of that angle; likewise, a logarithm is a function of the number it represents. In an ordinary algebraic equation, y is a function of $x\chi$ if y's value changes when the value of χ changes.

The year he died was 1650, when Descartes' colleagues had already begun to flesh out the bones of his book *La Geometric*. At that time an eight-year-old named Isaac Newton was flying kites with lanterns in them to scare the villagers of North Witham in Lincolnshire, England. And this child, scant years later, was to turn analytic geometry into the most practical mathematics ever invented—calculus, the mathematics of movement.

Then, in 1665 and 1666, England's incomparable Isaac Newton produced a prodigious brain child, now called calculus, which for the first time permitted the mathematical analysis of all movement and change. In calculus Newton combined the fine-slicing technique of the Greeks and the graph system of Descartes to devise a marvelously automatic mental tool for operating on an equation in order to get at infinitesimal. So quickly did calculus prove its effectiveness that in a few years its creator used it to work out the laws of motion and gravitation—the fundamental laws of physics which explain why the solar system acts as it does, or why any moving object reacts as it does to outside forces like gravity, the tension of a spring or the push of a man's hand. By its ability to probe the fleeting mysteries of movement, calculus today has become the principal pipeline between practical science and the reservoir of mathematical thought. Every airplane, every television set, every bridge, every bomb, every spacecraft owes it a tithe of indebtedness.

The different kinds of change which calculus can analyze are as diverse as a queen's wardrobe. If the factors involved in any fluid situation can be put in terms of an equation, then calculus can get at them and uncover the laws they obey. The change under scrutiny may be as dramatic as the gathering speed of a missile lifting from its pad or as quiet as the varying grade of a mountain road. it may be as visible as the pounds added around a once-svelte waistline or as invisible as the ebb and flow of current in a power line. It may be as audible as the crescendo of a Beethoven concerto or as silent as the buildup of flood force water behind a dam.

Calculus analyzes all these situations by invoking two new mathematical processes—the first fundamental operations to be added to the canon of mathematics since the laws of addition, subtraction, multiplication, division and finding roots were laid down some 4,000 years ago. These new operations are called *differentiation* and *integration*, and they are the reverse of each other in much the same way that subtraction is the reverse of addition, or division of multiplication. Differentiation is a way of computing the rate at which one variable in a situation changes in relation to another at any point in a process—at a given instant in time, for example, or at a given point in space. The actual method employed in differentiation is to divide a small change in one variable by a small change in another; to let these changes both shrink until they approach zero; then—and this is the key— to find the value which the ratio between them approaches as the changes become indefinitely small. This value is what mathematicians call a "limit," and it is the answer they are seeking, the end result of differentiation—the rate of change at a given instant or point. Integration works back the other way from differentiation; it takes an equation in terms of rate of change and converts it into an equation in terms of the variables that do the changing.

Through differentiation, a mathematician can probe deep into a fluid situation until he finds some unchanging factor that reflects the action of a constant law of nature. In this fashion Newton and later theorists made a discovery which is still not easy for laymen to absorb. This discovery was that the constant factor in many processes of nature is the rate at which a rate of change changes. Deciphering this seeming double talk may appear hopeless. But anyone who drives a car is familiar with the rate of change of a rate of change whether he realizes it or not. The speed of the car—so many miles per hour—is a rate of change of distance with respect to time. In speeding up or slowing down, the car's speed itself changes, and changes at a rate—acceleration or deceleration—which is the rate of change of the rate of change.

In nature, gravity acts to make a falling object move at a rate which increases at a constant rate. For processes involving actual physical movement, Newton defined this rate of a rate as the *acceleration*. And he called the gravity causing it a *force*. He defined force in general as something which causes an object to accelerate. As applied through calculus, this definition—laid down three centuries ago—has enabled scientists to do no less than identify the three fundamental forces of the cosmos: the force of gravitation; the force of magnetism, or électric charge; and the force that binds together the atomic nucleus.

In contrast to the spectacular role that calculus has played in unlocking the secrets of the universe, the nomenclature surrounding differentiation and integration is woefully prosaic. The relative change of a y or χ, found by differentiation, is called a *derivative*—a derivative of y with respect to χ, written $dy/d\chi$, or of χ with respect to y, written $d\chi/dy$. A derivative's counterpart, found by integration, is called an *integral*, and is symbolized by $\int$, an old-fashioned letter S, which was short, originally, for "sum" or "summation." When integration is performed on an equation written in terms of derivatives, it converts the equation back into one in which the χ and y have doffed their rate-of-change disguises and resumed normal algebraic appearance.

When used abstractly in an equation, a derivative can most readily be thought of in terms of the curve which represents this equation on a graph. At any point, the curve is rising or falling at a rate of so many y-units per χ-unit. This slope up or down is the exact geometric equivalent of the rate of change—the derivative—of y with respect to χ. Engineers often express the grade of a hill, the pitch of a roof or the steepness of an airplane's climb in identical terms : as so much altitude gained per unit of horizontal distance traversed. But in these applications the slope is normally conceived of as being measured over some definite span of distance. In calculus, on the other hand, the derivative is thought of as an instantaneous slope at a single point on a curve.

That this elusive concept of instantaneous slope is no figment of the mathematical imagination can be seen in an artillery shell as it arcs toward target. At any single moment the shell is moving in a definite direction. This direction is an instantaneous slope with respect to the ground, a rate of change in the shell's altitude with respect to its horizontal position. In terms of a graph, the speed of the shell, moving up or down, can also be considered as an instantaneous slope on a curve—a rate of change in the shell's altitude with respect to the time that has been elapsing in the shell's altitude with respect to the time that has been elapsing since the shell was fired. A mathematician would normally write such a derivative—the velocity of climb or fall, or the rate of change of vertical distance—as dy/dt, in which the t stands for time.

The counterpart of a derivative, an integral, can also be visualized in terms of a graph. Suppose that y equals some expression of χ and that this equation is plotted as a curve. Then the integral of y is the area between the curve and the horizontal line, or axis, running along below it.

To work out the rules of calculus, Newton visualized what would happen if one point on a graph-curve slid down into a point nearby. As the slide begins, the average slope of the curve between the two points is the number of y-units separating them vertically, divided by the number of x-units separating them horizontally. As the slide continues, both distances in this fraction diminish toward zero and finally vanish when the two points merge. But this does not mean that the fraction itself vanishes. A ratio of 1:2, for instance, need not suddenly become zero just because its numerator and denominator become indefinitely small. When last heard from, as they disappear arm in arm into the fastnesses of infinity, the numerator may be one zillionth and the denominator two zillionths, but the ratio between them is still 1 to 2.

Finding the value which a fraction approaches as its numerator and denominator both diminish toward nothingness is called "taking a limit." If the numerator equals half the denominator, the limit is 10. As two points on a curve slide together, the vertical and horizontal distances between them remain coupled, even as they fade away, by the relationship of y to χ expressed in the original equation of the curve. As they merge, therefore, the ratio of their distances approaches a definite limit which can be evaluated in terms of y and χ. This limit, 1/2 or 10 or whatever it may be, is the slope of the curve at the precise spot where the two points merge—the rate of change of vertical y with respect to horizontal χ or, put another way, the derivative of y with respect to χ.

The subtle train of reasoning which enabled Newton to differentiate equations and find the derivative or limiting value of the ratio—written $dy/d\chi$ or dy/dt—is the fundamental process of calculus. It can be roughly paraphrased as follows : In a developing situation, the difference between the state of affairs at one moment and the state of affairs at the next moment is an indication of how the situation is shaping up; and if the ratio of the net changes that take place between the two moments is evaluated as a limit—a limit approached when the interval between the two moments is imagined as diminishing toward zero—then that limit shows how fast developments are taking place. The logic of calculus can be applied to moments of time, points on a curve. temperatures in a gas or any state of affairs which can be related by equations; the same rules of differentiation apply to all of them.

The way these rules work, and the reason for their enormous usefulness, can best be illustrated by applying them to the classically simple equation $y=16t^2$, first expressed in a much simpler form by the physicist Galileo Galilei. This brief, unpretentious expression is one of the most useful in all physics because it shows how gravity acts on a freely falling object—an elevator run a much, a hailstone or a jumper descending to ground. Since almost all movements and changes on earth are heavily influenced by gravity, the equation of free fall indirectly plays a part in innumerable human actions—from taking a step or lobbing a tennis ball to lifting a steel girder or launching an astronaut into orbit.

Timing an object as it falls from a given height is the most straightforward method of gauging the effects of gravity. It was this technique which Galileo used, about 1585, to arrive at his free-fall equation. According to legend, Galileo dropped small cannon balls from the colonnades of the leaning tower of Pisa. According to his own account, he used the less fanciful means of timing bronze balls as they rolled down a ramp. The results of Galileo's experiments subsequently led to the equation for free fall, $y=16t^2$, with y representing the distance fallen in feet and t the elapsed time in seconds after the start of the fall.

By differentiating this equation twice—so as to shave away successive layers of change and inconstancy—Newton uncovered the essential nature of gravitation. Differentiating the equation once, he found that the speed with which a jumper is falling at any moment equals 32 times the number of seconds which he has been falling. Differentiating the equation a second time, he found that the jumper's acceleration—the rate of increase in his speed—is always 32 feet (9.8m) per second, every second.

The fact that in the free-fall equation acceleration equals a constant number, 32, indicates the end of the trail. This 32 need not be differentiated further; it does not change, and its rate of change is zero. If represents a law of nature: that every free-falling object falls to earth with a constant acceleration of 32 feet per second, every second.

Having ascertained this fact by calculus, Newton was able to set his mathematical sights far beyond the earth and to deduce the law of universal gravitation—one of the most important results ever to be achieved by mathematics. It is the law which governs the movements of all celestial bodies—from human beings in orbit to entire systems of stars.

Not even the skillful coaxings of Halley could convince Newton to publish his calculus—not, that is, until another mathematician, the Gennan Gottfried Wilhelm von Leibniz, had independently re-created the entire mental machinery. Leibniz invented calculus 10 years after Newton, in 1675, and in 1684 published his account of it, 20 years before Newton was to given the first published explanation of his own version.

Although Newton accomplished far more with calculus than Leibniz did, Leibniz had a superior notation for it—one he polished so carefully that we still use it. It was Leibniz who first wrote derivatives as *dy/dx* or *dx/dy*—forms that suggest the fractional rate-of-change measurements to which they apply.

Gauging likelihoods has been a human preoccupation since time immemorial. Since the mid-17th Century it has also been a serious pursuit of the mathematician. Out of his researches into the subject has come an entire specialty of his profession—the mathematics of probability—and a way of computing chances which is much sharper than a layman's guesses. To the mathematician, probability is a percentage : the frequency with which one phenomenon takes place in relation to possible alternatives. When combined, the probabilities of particular events can be used to evaluate the chances of chains of events. To deal with such combinations, certain basic rules have been formulated; it is these rules which have come to be known as the laws of chance.

In serving science and business, the mathematics of probability has attained a status far above its origins. which were slightly on the seamy side. Probability theory was inspired by the inquiries of gamblers seeking some inside information to help them win at cards and dice. Those raffish Renaissance algebraists, Tartaglia and Cardano, both came up with shrewd analyses of gambling problems. But their work—too gamy, perhaps, for mathematicians, and too mathematical for gamblers—was largely forgotten. Probability as we know it today was launched, instead, by a trio of Frenchmen in the mid-17th Century : a high-living nobleman, the Chevalier de Méré, and two spare-time mathematicians, Blaise Pascal and Pierre de Fermat.

Pascal's enthusiasm was "projective" geometry—a geometry dealing with the perspective problems of drawing and with the shadow forms which geometric shapes, held at various angles, will cast when thrown upon a screen. Fermat was a jurist by profession. He created parts of analytic geometry independently of Descartes, but he is mainly remembered as one of the leading number theorists of all time, a reputation which he gained by moonlighting on quiet evenings at home after sessions in the local parliament.

In 1651 or 1652 De Méré and Pascal found themselves together on a trip to the town of Poitou. Searching about for a mutually interesting topic of conversation with which to lighten the journey, the worldly De Méré presented the spiritual Pascal with a mathematical problem which had fascinated sporting bloods since the Middle Ages : how to split the pot in a dice game that has to be discontinued. pascal pondered the problem for a couple of years and in 1654 relayed it to Fermat.

Out of the researches of Pascal and Fermat into various gambling situations has evolved the modern theory of probability—the laws of chance. The idea that chance is governed by laws may seem unconvincing to anyone persuaded of the rule of Lady Luck. But actually the laws of chance do not preclude the possibility that an individual will enjoy a stroke of luck. Nor do they deny the value of playing hunches. They begin to act as laws only when many instances are involved—many throws of the dice, many deals of the cards, many car collisions, many lifetimes. This aspect of probability is known as the *law of large numbers.*

Since events are frequently related—rather than independent or mutually exclusive—the both-and and either-or laws of probability carry important riders. The both-and law of two events is modified if the occurrence of the first event effects the chances of the second. For instance, the probability of drawing one of the 13 hearts in a 52-card deck is 13/52, or simply 1/4. But the chance of getting a heart on both the first and second draw from a deck is not 13/52 × 13/52. After one heart has been drawn and there are only 12 hearts and 51 cards left to choose from, the probability that a heart will turn up has decreased from 13/52 to 12/51. As a result, the both-and chances of drawing two hearts in a row have been reduced to 13/52 × 12/51. This modification of the both-and law is called the *law of conditional probability.*

A similar proviso attaches to the either-or law. If two events are not mutually exclusive, the combined chances of either one or the other coming to pass are equal to the sum of their separate chances minus the chance of their both occurring together.

One great difficulty in applying the laws of probability lies in determining all the possible ways in which an event can take place. In dice games the problem is only moderately hard. Each successive toss of one die, or each new die added to a set of dice being thrown together, multiplies the number of possibilities by six.

As a labor-saving device mathematicians have worked out rules that will tell them at a glance how many separate orders or arrangements are concealed in any one set of possibilities. A set of possibilities—the five possible cards in a poker hand, for instance—is known mathematically as a "combination." Each way in which the cards can be arranged, or each order in which they can be drawn, is known as a "permutation."

The laws of permutations and combinations by which probability theorists make life easier for themselves have been arrived at through pondering the orders or arrangements which can come out of a hat—any kind of lottery drawing or card dealing.

The probability curve on graphs was first recognized and used by the mathematician Abraham de Moivre, a French Huguenot who had fled to England after the revocation of the Edict of Nantes in 1685. It was further developed by the 19th Century's dean of mathematics, Carl Friedrich Gauss. To represent the curve Gauss wrote an equation which is of signal usefulness to the scientist because it is couched in terms of the factors which come into play in experimental situations. If, for instance, the scientist wishes to know what chance there is that the measurements he has made in an experiment are for some reason atypical and perhaps unreliable, Gauss's equation tells him what the chance is of the measurements being wrong by 1 per cent or by any other percentage. As a result the scientist knows "the probable limit of error" in his work and can act accordingly. Gauss's equation also helps statisticians judge whether a piece of information is meaningful or merely fortuitous.

Since the time of Gauss, probability experts have worked up other equations and other curves to fit various kinds of situations not covered by the normal-distribution curve. Such so-called "abnormal" situations would include, for instance, the chances of dialing a wrong number, or the chances of your home being hit during an air raid. The note of gambling persists in these sophisticated applications of probability, but it has been transposed upward to new octaves of usefulness and respectability.

Mathematics, is in the thick of modern life. Never before has an ivory tower cast so long a shadow over the everyday world. At the same time, paradoxically, its initiates have not repented of their penchant for the abstract. They have made themselves at home in the wild blue yonder staked out by 19th Century mathematics. And there they now consort with abstractions of abstractions, with "covariants" and "contravariants," "transformation groups" and "transfinite numbers," "discontinuous deformations" and "topological spaces."

Such excursions into pure mathematical fancy, although they seem hopelessly impractical, have an odd way of running ahead of physical science, of supplying equations that fit the facts before science stumbles onto facts that fit the equations. This has happened so many times—and also failed to happen so many times—that many mathematicians see themselves as formulators of possibilities rather than as discoverers of truth. The license imparted by this "art-for-art's-sake" outlook has resulted in a prodigal inventiveness. Like the hordes and horses of some fabulous khan, today's mathematicians have ridden off in all directions at once, conquering faster than they can send messages home."

Scholars who have tried to keep track of this rampaging expansion assure us that we are living in the Golden Age of mathematics; they estimate that almost as much new mathematics has been created in this century as in all previous centuries combined. Statistics bear them out.

In both range and remoteness, modern mathematics defies easy description. In general, however, it has developed along-two lines: on the one hand success and conquest—the ability to solve problems; on the other hand soul-searching and contemplation—an uncertainty as to the nature and aim of ultimate mathematical abstractions. Both these strands are woven into the many-splendored fabric of mathematics today.

On the contemplative side, two of the most notable developments are set theory and symbolic logic. Set theory, among other things, provides a new kind of arithmetic for dealing with infinity; symbolic logic is an attempt to reduce all human reasoning to a mathematical notation. Both set theory and symbolic logic are abetted by a third form of mathematics, group theory, which plays a unifying role in analysis and reveals unexpected similarities between different mathematical domains.

Among its major conquests, 20th Century mathematics counts two whole new kingdoms: game theory and topology. Game theory is the analysis of strategy, whether in the hot games of business or the cold games of war. Topology is the study of the properties of geometric shapes which do not change when the shapes themselves are stretched, twisted, scrunched up or tuned inside out.

Of all the practical triumphs of mathematics, the most spectacular has been Relativity, which, in heralding our nuclear age, has irrevocably proved the awesome power that mathematics can wield over everyday life. The Theory of Relativity, Einstein's masterwork, is really two theories : Special Relativity and General Relativity, the former published in 1905, the latter in 1916. Both theories are based on the premise that all scientific measurements are relative to the reference frame of the beholder : that there is no fixed center in the cosmos for scientists to start from in measuring off distances and describing exactly where and when anything takes place in space.

In effect, Special Relativity is a rewrite of the equations of Newtonian mechanics to correct their inadequate descriptions of energy and of objects—distant galaxies or atomic particles—which move at nearly the speed of light, 186,000 miles per second (300 km/s). The portentous equation of nuclear power, $E=mc^2$ (which means that energy, E, in a piece of matter amounts to the mass, m, of the matter times the square of the enormous speed of light, c), came out of Special Relativity as a corollary.

General Relativity pursued the same theme as Special Relativity—but with a vengeance. In Special Relativity, Einstein had overhauled Newtonian laws so that they would apply to fast-moving bodies traveling with *steady* speeds along *straight* lines. In General Relativity he broadened his equations so that they would apply to bodies traveling with *changing* speeds along *curved* lines. These so-called "field equations" of General Relativity not only cover every possible state of motion but also describe the over-all behavior of our universe and other conceivable universes past, present or future. The reach of the equations—a few difficult symbols tantamount to entire books of philosophy—staggers the mind and beggars the imagination.

To work his wonders, Einstein arrayed the moving matter and energy of the cosmos within a mathematical framework of four dimensions : three for space and one for time. He included time because he had found in Special Relativity that time and space are inseparable—that the time at which an event occurs is not independent of the motion of the observer. In Einstein's later speculations, matter and gravity are manifestations of each other; thus matter can be thought of as an infusion of gravity, varying in strength from point to point. In the Unified Field Theory, Einstein attempted to explain electrical and magnetic forces.

To explore the labyrinths where future giants of knowledge may crouch, modern mathematicians light their way by the set theory, group theory and symbolic logic mentioned earlier. Group and set theory are both used to compare the tools of different branches of mathematics and to make them as freely interchangeable as possible. A set is any collection of entities, whether whole numbers, nut-brown maidens or egg-heads with horn-rimmed glasses. A group is a particular kind of set : of numbers symbols, points, lines, movements, atoms, units of energy or undefined what chamacallits. It is distinguished from just any old set by having to obey certain rules in regard to some operation like addition or multiplication. For instance, the offspring of any two members of the set, when they are combined by the operation, must remain in the set—the "4" produced by the wedding of "2" and "2" is also a whole number. Moreover, when several members of the set are combined by the operation, the way in which they are bracketed must not affect the result—for instance, *a (bc)* must equal *(ab)c*.

Set theory was developed by the German mathematician Georg Cantor as a technique for "anatomizing the infinite." During the 19th Century there had been stustained attempts to define processes like differentiation and integration in terms of simple arithmetic. The feeling was that if all processes and symbols could be so defined there would be less difficulty in reasoning accurately about them. As one mathematician, Leopold Kronecker, put it : "The whole numbers has the Dear God made. All else is man's work."

It was Cantor's triumph, in set theory, to distinguish different orders of infinity in different infinite sets. He compared infinite sets by pairing off their members, two by two, like the animals boarding Noah's ark or the teeth of a zipper being zipped up. By this seemingly simple method, he reached some astonishing conclusions. For instance, all the fractions can be matched off against the infinite set of all the whole numbers. The two infinite sets are thus "equal", yet the set of all fractions includes the set of all whole numbers by virtue of terms such as 2/1 or 6/2; in other words, though the two sets are equal, one contains the other as a "subset" By the same technique, Cantor found that other infinite sets—all the points on a line segment, for instance—cannot be matched off against the whole numbers. In short they cannot be counted; the points are infinitely more infinite than the whole numbers. Cantor found other orders of infinity—other "transfinite numbers"—which are still more infinite. He created an arithmetic for handling such infinite sets—a weapon, as it were, with which mathematicians could cut their age-old bugaboo of infinity down to several logical sizes.

Although sets are more inclusive than groups, group theory has been called the supreme art of mathematical abstraction. Its principal pioneer was a tragic young 19th Century Frenchman, Evariste Galois. Poor Galois launched group theory for equations as a precocious teenager beset by the disapproval of his elders. He recorded the bulk of his life's work in an almost unintelligible, 31-page document scribbled during the last night of his life, when he was just 20. The next morning he died in a senseless duel over politics and a girl he hardly knew.

Group theory gets to the bottom of what happens when one kind of mathematical operation is performed on different elements, or when different operations are successively performed on a single element. By such analysis it lays bare basic structural patterns in mathematics. An innovator stumped by difficulties can sometimes use group theory to cross over into other branches of mathematics and borrow tools, methods or simply precedents which enable him to push ahead with his work. The theory also helps scientists when they glimpse patterns darkly in nature. It has been used, for instance, to analyze configurations of molecules and crystals—arrangements important in the chemistry of human genes or in the "solid circuits" of sophisticated electronics.

All manner of mathematical objects behave as groups. For instance, an equilateral triangle can sit on any of its three sides and still look the same. The rotations that carry the triangle from one of these positions to another constitute a group. What is more, this group has a structural counterpart in a certain group of permutations and in a group formed by the solutions to a particular cubic equation. All three groups are realizations of a single "abstract group." Thus the same abstract group covers cases from three separate realms : geometry, the arithmetic of arrangements and algebra. In abstract groups the most unlikely scions of mathematics turn out to be close kin—the same abstract logic masquerading under different disguises.

The deft changes which group theory works on one kind of mathematical creature to make it into some other kind of creature are known as "transformations." An algebraic equation is transformed when, for example, every x in it is replaced by a y—5. A geometric figure in a plane is transformed when it is stretched or when its shadow is projected onto a different surface or into a different kind of space. It was a group of algebraic transformations, devised by a Dutch physicist, Hendrik A. Lorentz, to deal with certain problems in electricity, which Einstein seized hold of in constructing Special Relativity.

During transformations some aspect of an equation or of a geometric shape may remain stubbornly unchanged. Such solid islands are called "invariants." They may be no more noticeable than the invariant twinkle in the eye of a stock-company actor who plays Hamlet and Professor Higgins on alternate nights, but mathematicians seek them out and cling to them because they provide the most significant clues of all to underlying identities. An ideal of the importance attached to them can be gleaned from a group-theory definition of geometry as "the study of the invariants of geometric configurations under groups of transformations."

The most introspective of the supermaths which help 20th Century analysts find their way is symbolic logic : a notation for stating and manipulating all sorts of propositions so as to bring both sequiturs and non sequiturs into mercilessly sharp relief. Through symbolic logic—whose flavor can be sampled in the extract from Lewis Carroll —mathematicians have undertaken a Sisyphean task : to classify and analyze the thoughts involved in every branch of mathematics, with the aim of identifying the axioms and procedures at the base of each and of reducing all possible proofs to the barest skeletons. By this plan the results should be absolutely abstract and clear-cut statements like "if axiom A is granted then theorem B follows," which in one symbolic logical script would be written as A   B, or "if either A or B is granted then the negative of C follows," which would be set down as AvB   ~C. Several monumental efforts have been made to translate all mathematical reasoning into such revealing shorthand—most notably in the three symbol-heavy tomes of the Principia Mathematica, published by Alfred North Whitehead and Bertrand Russell between 1910 and 1913.

Symbolic logic has produced one of the most curious and influential theorems in all modern mathematics. This is Gödel's Proof, an extremely abstract line of reasoning which shows that no useful branch of mathematics can be constructed on a consistent set of axioms themselves. It is as if some structural property of a right triangle were forever unverifiable by the Euclidean axioms which lead to the Pythagorean theorem. For arithmetic Gödel's

Proof demonstrates that all the possible relationships between whole numbers cannot be deduced from any one set of basic assumptions. The possible relationships or "truths" about numbers are as unlimited as the parade of numbers itself. For mathematics as a whole, the implication is that the subject will never be complete—that there is limitless scope for fishing in the mathematical ocean.

Kurt Gödel—a member of the Institute for Advanced Study at Princetor—worked out his remarkable theorem in 1931 when he was 25 years old. He demonstrated it by what is called an "existence proof"— an argument which shows that something exists without necessarily producing the something for inspection. Gödel's theorem is variously regarded with antipathy or exhilaration. Those most hurt are the "formalist" mathematicians who had hoped to establish each branch of mathematics once and for all on a single consistent set of axioms. Those most gladdened are the freewheeling spirits who cannot endure the thought that mathematics will ever be cut and dried. One of the greatest of these was the late John Von Neumann, who played a leading role in the development of the atomic bomb. Von Neumann once said, "Much of the best mathematical inspiration comes from experience and......it is hardly possible to believe in the existence of an absolute immutable concept of mathematical rigor dissociated from all human experience."

One of Von Neumann's own major contributions, the theory of games, is one of the most practical mathematical developments of our time. it propounds intricate laws of strategy : how to adopt the best variations in play to avoid being beaten by a shifty adversary; how to make the best of a bad situation or avoid the worst of a good situation when faced by a fully rational, fully analytic competitor of known means and resources.

Game theory has been put to a gamut of uses. It has helped to determine the most profitable length of time a record company should wait between the releases of two sure-fire hit recordings; it has been employed, in a "blue-sky," or "think," contract let not long ago by the Office of Naval Research, to analyze the mathematical structure of competitive "American-type" economies. In a game that offers no clear-cut way of winning, game theory can show how to find the strategy which will come closest to achieving a stalemate. As a result, the idea of minimized maximum losses—called "minimaxes" or "saddle points" by Von Neumann—has been taken up by both camps in the Cold War.

Between the difficult abstract logic of the formalists and the equally difficult theories of the Von Neumanns in modern mathematics falls the shadow of the high-speed electronic computers. Day by day, mathematics is being translated from elegant formulas into prosaic instruction sheets which the computers digest by mechanical brute force. A computer can solve problems which would leave a Newton or a Gauss gaping, and solve them to any number of decimal places, by purely pragmatic schemes of approximation, of endless try-try-and-try-again arithmetic.

Meanwhile pure mathematicians are climbing ever higher into new skies of abstraction. What they are accomplishing none of us really knows, because the equivalents of Relativity and atomic energy which may grow out of the mathematics of today may not be realized for decades.

BRANCHES OF MATHEMATICS

How many languages do we know? Just one? Perhaps we are learning one or two more now. We may know a few words in several different languages : names of things to eat, songs, how to say 'please' and 'thank you' or a prayer. Families that have strong ties with other countries of cultures often speak a second language at home. If we answered the question quickly, we probably did not think of including what we know of a very special language. Everyone in the world knows at least a little of it. People need it in some way every day. No business could be done without its help. Every shop and store in the world would close at once if it did not exist. What is this universal language?, That is Mathematics.

Mathematics uses numbers, signs, shapes and patterns instead of words. In other languages, the rules of grammar show us how to put words in the right form and the right order so we can express our ideas and link them together. Grammar is like a skeleton that holds together and gives shape to the words we use when we speak, read or write. Mathematics is just like that too. It has clear rules that show how numbers, spaces, patterns and many other things can be joined together, separated, combined and changed to describe and explain ideas.

A baby learns language step by step. A very small baby cannot use much language or explain itself easily. Often only its parents can understand it. As it grows, it learns from the world around it. Schools teach special language skills like reading and writing. Eventually the child becomes an adult who can speak easily about anything. Everyone who knows the language can understand what is being said. We learn mathematics in much the same way. We can see many of its basic ideas in every day life. Pouring water into different shaped jugs teaches us something about measuring. Counting different sorts of fruits on a table introduces numbers and sets. Cutting out paper snowflakes for a festival decorations introduces mathematical symmetry. At school, we learn more about these ideas and how to use them. Eventually, as our skills improve, we find we can explain difficult ideas very neatly and precisely using mathematics, not words.

People interested in science study mathematics until they can use it comfortably at a highly complicated level. Scientists work to understand, describe and sometimes control many things that happen in the language for their work. A chemist, for example, wants to know precisely what happens when he mixes two chemicals together. Will they do something useful or something dangerous? How much of each does he need to achieve the same results again and again? A doctor testing a new drug must know how much is safe to use. What pattern of events occurs when the drug is used on animals in the laboratory? Physicists, trying to understand what happens inside an atom, the smallest unit of matter in the universe, need mathematics to express what they discover.

People who study the applied sciences such as engineering, also need good mathematical understanding. Mathematics helps someone design a beautiful and strong bridge or an efficient engine. In business and banking, mathematics helps people make decisions. Because mathematics is so important and useful, it is said that too many people stop studying it at an early age. When this happens, they often find themselves stuck, like a child that has not grown up, able to understand only a few ideas and use just the basic, least interesting skills.

Numbers

Mathematics begins with numbers. All languages in the world have words for numbers. But what exactly is a number? A number is a symbol-such as four of 4-that stands for a particular 'how many' or shows us precisely where something belongs in a list or sequence of things. Mathematics today uses many symbols, different marks or signs that have a special meaning—but numbers are the most ancient ones and the ones we learn first.

When ancient people began to use numbers they noticed that there is a wonderful order about them. Patterns of numbers can be repeated perfectly again and again if the same numbers are combined or separated in the same way. Numbers were more exact than ordinary words to describe the size and shape of things. Philosophers noticed that if they wanted to think about quantities or how things could relate to each other, numbers helped them think clearly and precisely. They also came to see that there were many different kinds of numbers and these could be arranged in different systems and used in different ways.

The numbers we know best, the series that begins 1,2,3,4,........, are called whole numbers. Another name for them is integers. Although we now write them very differently from the way they were written by the Egyptians, Greeks and Romans, each number today is used in exactly the same way as it was then. We use whole numbers in different ways but chiefly for counting. It does not matter what we want to count, large or small, alive or not. We count sheep the same way we count bricks.

We group our numbers in tens; our system is called the decimal system—the ten system—and we know it well as we count our money in it. Other people have used different groupings; the Romans grouped their numbers in fives, and Babylonians in sixties. Computers are based on a grouping in twos, called the binary system.

Sometimes we need to think about negative quantities. We may need to describe how air can be colder than ice, for example. Mathematicians give us a way to do this too. They invented a way of writing 'nothing', by using 'zero'; Not only does zero (or nought) make it easy to deal with large numbers but it can also be used to divide all numbers into two groups, positive and negative.

Negative numbers are easy to understand if we imagine all the whole numbers in the universe written in an unending line. Put zero in the middle of the line. The numbers on the right increase and are positive, the numbers on the left decrease and are negative. We will also notice that there are gaps between each dot. We have all measured something and found that it is not quite, or just a little bit more than, a whole number. Mathematics has a special number system to cope with this problem too.

Rational numbers are those we use to describe the relationship—the ratio— between one whole number and another whole number. An integer is one kind of rational number : some examples of integers written as ratios are 'proper' fractions, such as 1/2 are also rational numbers, and fit in between the whole numbers.

Mathematicians have discovered some other numbers that are not rational and cannot be expressed as the ratio between two integers. These are called irrational numbers. An example is the number which says how many times you have to multiply the diameter of a circle to find its circumference; this number starts off as 3.14159..... and goes on for ever.

Another special number system, imaginary numbers, has been invented to deal with the problem of finding a number which, when multiplied by itself, gives a negative answer. Imaginary numbers are very useful to physicists when they try to describe such things as how energy works.

Arithmetic

Arithmetic introduces most of us to formal mathematics. With numbers, arithmetic uses four basic operations : addition, subtraction, multiplication and division. As we do different sorts of calculations--working out problems using numbers—we learn how to use those operations. We begin in a simple way, using small whole numbers. Then we learn how to handle larger numbers and complicated calculations that may use two or more operations to complete. We progress to fractions and decimals. Arithmetic prepares us for some of the more advanced mathematical ideas and skills we will meet in other branches of mathematics such as algebra and trigonometry.

The basis of all arithmetic is classification : sorting things into groups of alike or unlike numbers. From classification, we can count how many things there are in a group (enumeration); how many things in several groups are of different sizes (addition); how many things in several groups are of the same size (multiplication); we can compare different sized groups (subtraction); we can split a large group into several smaller groups all the same size as each other (division). We discover the relationships between addition, multiplication, subtraction and division. Multiplication is a kind of fast addition; subtraction is a kind of backward addition—what must we add to a smaller number to obtain a larger one? Division is the opposite of multiplication : if 5 children have 6 sweets each, altogether they have 5×6=30 sweets; if you want to hare a bag of 30 sweets equally between 5 children, they would each get 30÷5=6.

In the past, primary school mathematics usually dealt only with basic arithmetic. Classes were boring. Children spent long hours practising addition, multiplication, subtraction and division-especially 'long' division, dividing one very large number by another large number. But not much time was spent on discussing how to tackle real problems which need arithmetic, so often children did not know whether they should be adding or multiplying. Now-a-days we have calculators to do the slog work of 'sums', and spend a lot of time on making sure that pupils know what to do solve a problem. A calculator is the modern aid to calculation but there have always been such aids, for example the abacus and Napier's bones.

Even though we use calculators, it is still very important that we know all our easy number patterns and our tables. By a 'number pattern' we mean results that keep cropping up that help us to check our work : 3 plus 7 is 10; 13 plus 7 is 20; 23 plus 47 is 70: can you see a pattern? (If we add any two numbers that end in 3 and 7 our answer will always end in 0—if it is correct!) For the same reason we must know the multiplication tables; it is easy to make a small mistake on a calculator and enter a wrong number, but knowing the tables makes it easier to spot the error when checking the answer.

When we use calculators we must always ask ourselves at the end if our answer makes sense. A calculator display of our answer may show a lot of noughts after the other figures, and we must know if our answer is to be in the tens, or hundreds, or thousands. Suppose you want to know how long it will take you to drive 126 miles at an average speed of 42 miles an hour : your calculator may show the answer as 300,00,000—how many of those noughts do you need ? Do you need any? Before putting the sum on the calculator, ask yourself 'Are there some easier numbers that are near to the ones I have to use? Suppose the problem was 120 miles at

40 miles an hour. How many 40s in 120? 3. So the answer to the problem is going to be something like 3, and not 30 or 300.

It is a very good habit to look around you and try to 'estimate' or make a sensible guess at the size of things around you; how tall is the coconut tree in your garden? If you cannot guess, reason it : is it taller than a man? How many men standing on each others' shoulders would reach the top? Probably two, and then a little bit more. How tall is a man? A bit less than 1.8m (6ft.). So two men and a bit make about 3.5m to 4 m (12 ft or 13 ft.), which gives you a good idea of the height of your coconut tree.

Algebra

Algebra takes us farther into the world of mathematical thought. It uses numbers but has other symbols as well, chiefly letters of the alphabet, especially x. The symbols make it possible for us to investigate unknown numbers or quantities. If you tell someone you need five apples to make a pudding and are going to buy two more but do not say how many you already have, you could not write that down in arithmetic. In algebra you can, by saying $x + 2 = 5$. The x stands for the unknown number of apples you already have. In more complicated problems with several unknowns, other letters of the alphabet are used.

More varied and complicated problems can be set over clearly in algebra because it has a richer symbolic language than arithmetic. The familiar plus and minus signs are used for addition and subtraction but multiplication and division are indicated differently. To show that two numbers are to be multiplied we place them side by side with no symbol between them. For example 3a means 3 times whatever number a stands for. Also xy means that the number y stands for is multiplied by the number x represents. If we need to say that a number must be multiplied by itself several times, this is easily done by using a small number put slightly above and to the right of the main number, x^2. The small number is called an exponent. X^2 thus means x times x. Division is indicated by fractions. When we see it means that whatever x stands for is divided by 3.

When we want to compare things, algebra has special symbols to show whether one thing is the same size, larger than, or smaller than, another. The first symbol we recognize from arithmetic, = which means 'equals'. The other two are > which means 'is larger than' and < which means 'is smaller than'.

Equations are statements in algebra where the total value on the left of the equal sign must be exactly the same as that on the right. An inequality is another kind of algebraic statement. It can be true for many values of an unknown number whereas an equation is true only for certain values. When people talk about solving equations, they mean they work out what the unknowns stand for. Some equations can have several correct solutions. This makes them very different from ordinary calculations in arithmetic.

Algebra is particularly helpful in problem solving. First you put together an equation that correctly describes the problem. Sometimes just one equation will not be enough and several are needed. These are called simultaneous equations and they can often be worked out using a graph. To be able to solve equations will not be enough and several unknown quantities, there must be as many equations as there are unknowns. If there are four unknown quantities, you must have four equations; otherwise you will not be able to find values for all the unknowns.

Geometry

If arithmetic and algebra provide the hard-working grammar of mathematics, geometry—for all its usefulness— adds a dash of art and philosophy. Geometry describes, compares and makes it possible for us to measure all the different shapes we see around us. Stop and think for a moment just how many there are. Some are flat with edges. Some are round. Some are thick and can be filled with other things of different shapes of something that can alter its shape, like water. Even living things like plants and animals have shapes that can be described geometrically.

Being able to measure shapes is very important. Everyone needs to do it in some way at some time or other. Farmers and builders need to know how much land there is in a field to judge if they have enough for what they want to do. Anyone with a house needs to know how to work out how much carpeting to buy, how much paint will cover a wall, or how many tiles will cover the bathroom floor. Even the manager of super-market will be helped by geometry because its rules will reveal how many and what sort of packages and containers will stick together for an attractive display and not fall down. Nearly two thousand years before

Columbus set off on his famous voyage to prove the world was round, Greek mathematicians using their knowledge of geometry had worked out that the world was a sphere-shaped like an orange.

Like arithmetic, geometry uses 'classification', sorting shapes into different groups by seeing what properties they have in common, and where they differ. One classification is of all those shapes that are flat, have straight sides and sharp corners. We call this group 'polygons'. We can then divide the group of 'polygons into smaller groups : all the three-sided ones are called triangles. those with four sides are called quadrilaterals. We can then divide the smaller groups into still smaller groups : triangles with all the sides the same length are called 'equilateral' triangles; quadrilaterals with all sides equal and all the angles 'square' (or 'right angles) are called squares. Sorting shapes in this way shows us that all triangles and all squares are polygons, as they all belonged to the first sorting. or first classification. But the reverse is not true : not all polygons are triangles. So we have to be careful.

Another classification is of solid shapes where all the sides are polygons. These solides are called 'polyhedra'. You know the cube. which has six sides, each of which is a square. Do you know the tetrahedron, which has four sides, each of which is a triangle? Some cartons of milk, or of fruit juice, are made in this shape, as it is very difficult to tip over, and several of them can stick together with no spaces in between. Another classification is those shapes we get if we rotate a flat shape about its axis; a circle will rotate into a sphere; a square will rotate into a cylinder; a triangle will rotate into a cone.

In geometry we study the relationships between the different elements that make up shapes—the sides and angles of polygons, the area covered by a flat surface, the volume of a solid.

An important element in many shapes is the corners. To study corners we look at how much the line along one side of the corner has to turn or rotate about the corner so that it lies along the other line. We call this amount of turning an 'angle'. Stand on one spot and hold an arm out in front of you to point at something directly ahead. Now turn right round, in a full circle, so you are again pointing at that same object. To measure an amount of turning, first think of the full circle, you have just turned. Now imagine that instead of doing it in a smooth turn all at once, you had done it in a series of tiny jerks, 360° in all, all the same size. Each of these tiny jerky turns is called a 'degree'. A turn of a full circle is made up of 360 part turns, each of one degree. A turn of half a circle, so you are facing in the opposite direction to your original position, is made up of half of 360 degrees, that is, 180 degrees; a quarter turn, say from facing north to facing east, is made up of a quarter of 360 degrees, that is 90 degrees. If you stand straight with both arms pointing ahead of you, and then turn one arm so that it is pointing out to your side, that arm has made a turn 90 degrees, and there is a 'square' angle between your arms. The symbol denotes 'degree', and we write, for example, 90° or 180°. An angle of less than 90° is called an 'acute' angle, one between 90 and 180 is called 'obtuse' and one between 180° and 360° is called 'reflex'.

Many of the shapes, flat and solid, studied in geometry are symmetrical. This means that a line or cut through them can divide them into two equal parts. The cutting line, or it may be the folding line if the shape is made of cloth or paper, is called the axis of symmetry. Some shapes have more than one axis, a square has four. Two cuts the square into matching rectangles, two others divide it into equal triangles. A triangle whose sides are all exactly the same length or equal is called an equilateral triangle. It has three axes of symmetry (axes is the plural of axis). A circle, one of the most fascinating shapes, has an infinite number. This means you can draw an unlimited number of axes through its centre and still have equal halves.

Shapes that cannot be divided symmetrically are called asymmetric. But it is possible to make new symmetric shapes with them. Draw a triangle with each side a different length. Look at its reflection in a mirror. Although it has the same sides and angles, it looks different because it is back to front. Cut out the asymmetric triangle. Draw its reflection and cut it out. Put the triangles down side by side with two sides of equal length touching. That becomes an axis of symmetry. The new shape may have either three or four sides. If you do the experiment with a solid shape made out of clay or plasticine, the joining point is the plane of symmetry.

The parts of symmetrical shape or object are not just equal and balanced, they are mirror-images of each other. Our bodies are more or less symmetrical. You can understand the mirror image idea if you try to put your left hand on top of your right with both palms down. They won't match. Put your palms together and they will. All two-sided symmetry is called bilateral.

Another kind of symmetry is called rotational. It describes a shape that is unchanged in appearance when it is turned or rotated by a certain amount. A good example is the propeller of a small airplane, where three blends come from the central knob and the angle between each blade is 120°. When the propeller turns 120°, each blade moves into the position another has left so it looks exactly as it did before it began to move. Some shapes, like equilateral triangles, have both bilateral and rotational symmetry.

Symmetry is far more than a beautiful or curious geometric fact. Even the smallest clusters of matter, molecules, have different kinds of symmetry, and this affects the way they group together. Molecules of frozen water join together symmetrically to form snow flakes. Molecules of different sorts of chemicals join on their planes of symmetry to make useful crystals. In people, symmetry is often the basis for physical beauty. Often, when we say someone is beautiful, what we really mean is that their features and body have a perfect symmetry.

Topology

All the far reaches of modern mathematics, some of today's best minds are working in a strange world of fascinating, improbable shapes. this field is known as topology. It is a special kind of geometry concerned with the ways in which surfaces can be twisted, bent, pulled, stretched or otherwise deformed from one shape into another. Sometimes topologists deal with surfaces that no one could construct, sometimes they conceive of forms that seem impossible—e.g., a surface with only one side. Their special world of pure mathematics ranges from seeming child's play to difficult abstractions that leave even the experts puzzled. Topologists like to quote a parody of Hiawatha, about an Indian, who made some mittens of furry skin. "He, to get the warm side inside/Put the inside skin side outside" and "to get the cold side outside/put the warm side fur side inside." In his mitten-twisting, the Indian was in fact performing a topological manoeuver.

When a child picks up a ball of modelling clay, squeezes it into the shape of a box, then flattens it into a disk, he is performing topological transformations. What he has done is to deform the clay without breaking or tearing it. To a topologist, a figure thus transformed has not really changed at all.

All of the topological transformations involve a property known as genus of a surface. Roughly speaking, genus is defined according to the number of holes the object has—or, as the topologists say, by the number of non-intersecting closed or completely circular cuts that can be made on the surface without cutting it into two pieces.

Topologists enjoy creating odd shapes and strange objects. Among the most curious of these is the one-sided surface, introduced by the German mathematician and astronomer Augustus Ferdinand Mibius (1790—1868). Mibius described, in an article published after his death, his remarkable paper surface as a strip which has no other side. This one-sided strip, hard to imagine but easy to construct, has all kinds of unexpected properties. A Mobius strip is easily made from an ordinary flat strip of paper. First the strip is given a half twist and then the two ends are connected to make a closed ring. When a cut is made around the middle of a Mobius strip, it might be expected to divide the strip into two. But when a line is drawn around the strip and the strip is cut along the line, is not two strips but a two-sided strip. The mathematicians explanation to this is—A Mobius strip has but one edge, the out adds a second edge—and a second side. The Mobius strip cut one third of the way in from its edge produces a fresh surprise. The scissors make two complete trips around the strip but only a single continuous cut. The end result of this cut is two strips intertwined. One of the strips is a two-sided hoop and the other is a new Mobius strip, with its one continuous side bounded by a single edge. Another interesting aspect of a Mobius strip is—any one can paint an ordinary paper ring green on one side and red on the other. But, as one mathematician said, 'Not even Picasso could do that to a Mobius band'. If anyone tried, he would only prove that the strip has only one side—on which both colours must meet. About this phenomena a writer noted—"A mathematician confided/that a Mobius band is one-sided/And you'll get quite a laugh/If you cut one in half/For it stays in one piece when divided".

Another German mathematician, Felix Klein (1849—1925), following Mobius lead, devised a bottle with but one surface—i.e., it has an outside but no inside. Such a bottle, if it could be cut in half length-wise, would fall into two Mobius strips. The Klein bottle can become when the neck of tube goes inside and joins the base. A poet explained the stay of the Klein bottle as — "A mathematician named Klein/Thought the Mobius band was divine/said he 'If you give/The edges of two/You'll get a weird bottle like mine"

Topologists can make a distinction between the true mazes and figures like the Jordan curves. Topologically a Jordan curve is related not to the mazes but to the circles. It is merely a circle that has been twisted out of shape. Like a circle it still has an inside and outside—to get from one to the other, atleast one line must be crossed. This can be seen by following the paths from either or the dead ends at the center of the Jordan curve, one lane leads out of the curve. the other lane ends inside. Mazes are covered by another branch of topology, which is called network theory. Network theory provides a mathematical rule for getting out of any maze—but the rule itself is as complicated as a maze.

Network theory is one of the most practical forms of topology, with applications to electrical circuitry and economics. It was developed by Leonhard Euler (1707—1783), the grandfather of topology, who had solved two problems in topology 100 years before topology had been named. By sheer coincidence, both of the problems, which he thought unrelated, turned out to be part of what is now called network theory.

The two puzzles that interested Euler both concerned networks of lines connecting a number of points. The first involved the bridges of Koningsberg. It had been a tradition among the people that the seven bridges could not all be crossed in a continuous walk without re-crossing the route at some point, but no one knew the explanation. When Euler heard of the Koningsberg bridges, he realized that an important principle was involved in it, and he proceeded to demonstrate mathematically why such a work was impossible. The second of Euler's topological investigations concerned the many-sided objects known as polyhedra, which might be described as networks of points and lines in three dimensions. Studying these objects. Euler made a major discovery : No matter how many faces such a figure has, theory is a predictable relationship among the number of its points. edges and sides. This result is still known as "Euler's formula"

Trigonometry

How can we find out how tall a tree is without climbing to the top and letting down a measuring tape? How can we discover where we are in the middle of the ocean by looking at the sun? How can we calculate the height of a wall and the length of a ladder propped against it? The answer to these and many other questions, including how to aim a moon rocket, begins by saying : Use a triangle. It must be a 'right' triangle, that is one that has an angle of 90° at one of its points. The information it can provide will help you work out your problem quickly, using arithmetic and algebra as needed.

Triangles have many interesting properties; from the lengths of their sides and the size of their angles we can deduce other properties such as their area, or the size of the circle that goes through all of their points. Trigonometry, the study of triangles, has become a major branch of mathematics. In trigonometry we start by examining the relationships between the angles of a triangle, and the lengths of its sides. Trigonometry was developed during the times when sailors were exploring the world, crossing the Atlantic, sailing around Africa to India and China, sailing right around the world. They needed accurate ways of navigating, and finding where they were in the middle of vast oceans.

In tackling any mathematical problem, one of the first things to ask yourself is 'What do I knowin already? Can I use that to help me solve my problem?' Sailors realized that one of the things they could always know, or find out, at sea, was the angle which a pointer aimed at the sun made with the vertical. Trigonometry was the series of mathematical techniques they worked out so that this angle made by the sun would help them find their exact position.

They started by thinking about right angled triangles, that is, triangles where one angle is 90°. They chose this because the angle between the horizontal and the vertical is 90°. The geometry of the Greeks helped the sailors to realize that the ratios between pairs of sides would always be the same, so long as the angles of the triangle did not change; a triangle with longer sides but the same angles would give the same ratios. They gave names to these ratios: tangent, sine and cosine, usually written as tan, sin and cos.

Trigonometric tables show the values of tan, cos and sin for all possible angles (and calculators are now programmed with these values). Sailors first used a sextant to find out the angle of the sun at mid-day; they had also to know the date, because the sun's angle varies with the time of year and the time of day. Then, using trigonometric tables, they could work out their exact position. They had to be sure to take the measurements exactly at mid-day if the tables were to be used, and this meant that they had to have very exact clocks. That is why during the great period of world exploration in the 15th and 16th centuries, practical scientists spent a lot of time designing and perfecting accurate clocks.

Calculus

When the 17th century great mathematicians Isaac Newton and Gottfried Wilhelm von Leibniz developed calculus as a way of measuring motion, they were, in a sense, introducing to mathematics the principles of the motion picture. For just as a movie film consists of repeated still pictures of a moving object, so does calculus break motion down into stills that can be observed frame by frame. Once calculus was invented, mathematicians could treat a moving object as a point tracing a path through space and, by stopping the action, calculate the speed and acceleration of the object at a specific instant. This mathematics of motion became a fundamental scientific tool. The earth we stand on is in motion; so are the molecules of the air we breathe. With calculus, such movements can be defined even though they cannot be seen. Although some of its abstractions are as difficult as anything in mathematics, calculus is based on a few simple ideas—function, approximation, rate of change, convergence, and integration.

Function, common to many branches of mathematics, in central to calculus. when a point moves along a path, the distance it travels is a function of—i.e., depends on—the time it takes. In general, one variable is a function of another if a change in one depends on a change in the other—as a boy's height is a function of his age. This relationship can usually be written as an equation or drawn as a straight or curved line on a graph. Calculus can then be used to analyze the graph of a function—and thus the physical motion or change itself. The analysis of function is important because virtually everything in the world is undergoing some kind of transition. Metals, for example, expand when heated : thus the length of a brass bar is a function of its temperature. If its length when cold is known, the length when heated can be found once its temperature is determined. Another everyday function is the cost of sending a letter. Once the charge for 10 grams or a fraction thereof is known, the weight determines the among of postage needed, i.e., postage is the function of weight. Some other functions useful in the space age are the relationship of the speed of a satellite to the diameter of its orbit and the relationship of an astronaught's need for oxygen to his physical stress.

Change is inherent in this physical world and approximation is necessary at this point. Things take shape, grow, move, speed up. Most changes occur at uneven rates. An aeroplane picks up speed and raise faster toward the end of its climb than at the start. Just as it is possible to find the average rate of it is possible to find the average rate of the plane's rise by dividing the total weight of ascent by the time elapsed while rising, it is also possible to find the average rate of rise over any small interval, or frame of process. But calculus can go further. It can make these frames so small that each one approximates a single point—i.e., a single instant in time. It is then possible to determine the precise rate of change that is taking place at that instant.

Every shape that's born bears in its womb the seed of change. Among the many kinds of change in today's high-geared world, one of the most familiar is acceleration, which is vividly illustrated in the tensed muscles of runners, springing forward in a hundred-meter dash. The exact acceleration—or the rate of change of speed—at any one of the moments can be determined by depicting the entire ride in graph form. When such a graph is drawn, as in the case of a child's growth, certain information is reflected in the curve : Its unevenness, for example, reflects an uneven rate of growth from year to year. The rate of growth at any given point can be determined by drawing a line tangent to the curve,—i.e., touching it at only one point. The slope of the tangent line measures the precise rate of growth at the point where it touches. If the slant of the tangent is sleep, the rate of growth is rapid and if the tangent is horizontal, no growth is taking place at that point on the curve.

A fundamental concept of calculus is convergence to a limit—the idea that an unknown value can be measured by closing in through approximations that are made finer and finer until they are refined, in effect, to a precise value. The railway tracks converging on the horizon suggest this method : although they never meet in fact, they appear to get so close to a point that for all practical purposes they can be said to join at that point. Probably the best-known example of convergence is the 206-figure decimal expansion (pi=3.141 592 653 589 793 238 462 643 383 279 502 884 197

169 399 375 105 820 974 944 592 307 816 406 286 208 998 628 034 825 342 117 067 982 148 086 513 282 306 647 093 844 609 550 582 231 725 359 408 128 481 117 450 284 102 701 938 521 105 559 644 622 948 954 930 381 964 428 81). This is the value of pi—the ratio of any circle's circumference to its diameter—and although it has been carried elsewhere to more places, no one can ever reach the end. (A hundred years ago, William Shanks computed 'pi' to 707 decimal places working with paper and pencil for 20 years. In 1950, a computing machine computed 'pi' to 3000 decimal places in 13 minutes.) But by extending the decimal as far as we want, we can get as near to the true value of pi as we desire.

When some physical rate of change is graphed, the area under the curve has a special meaning. It represents the total of whatever value the curve represents. The technique by which the area under a curve is determined is called integration. There is no algebraic method for finding the area of such an odd-shaped figure, but calculus finds its precise are by filling it with rectangles of known area. These never completely fill the area under a curve, but the method of integration is to narrow the rectangles until the area they do not fill approaches zero. Then their total area is said to equal that under curve.

Statistics

Statistics prove 90% prefer TV programmes. Statistics say 92% will vote for pleasure. Statistics show a good chance for life in another galaxy! We all have heard or read statements like these. They make us suspect that statistics is just a numerical game played by people who want us to buy something, admire a certain politician or be amazed at something in the news. In fact, they are all examples of the misuse of statistics. Statistics is an important branch of modern mathematics, essential to all kinds of scientific research.

The earliest statistics were the facts governments collected about the number of people in a country, how old they were, where they lived, what kind of work they did, if they owned a house or a farm. These were 'facts of state'—the word statistics comes from this. Today governments everywhere spend a great deal of time and money collecting statistics about their citizens. The information can then be used to help planning and making decisions about things such as how many schools to build or where new roads are needed.

Government statistics are gathered in many ways but the most important is a census, an official survey of the citizens. These usually take place once every ten years in India.

Even very simple collections of statistics can be misleading. Readers may think the figures 'prove' one thing when they really 'prove' something very different. This happens because statistics, in addition to using very complex mathematical operations, uses ordinary words but in a very special scientific way.

When we say 'average' for example, we mean—unless we are speaking statistically—an arithmetical average. This is the sum of a list of numbers divided by the number of items in the list. The statistical idea of 'average' is more complex. The statistician has extra words like 'mode', 'median' and 'mean'. Each has some of our usual idea of average in it, but each is arrived at by a different mathematical process. Therefore each 'average' would be different.

The first operation in statistics is to collect data. Data is any quantifiable (that is something we can count or measure) information. How it is collected, how much is collected and sometimes even where and when it is collected may affect the results. Because we can collect information from only some of the people or things we are interested in, we choose a sample. For most statistical purposes—but not all—this is a random sample. That means that the people or items are selected in such a way that no one particular type appears to be chosen more often than another. In a factory, someone pulling a random sample of computers off a production line for a quality check will not select most of them from just one work-bench. Someone taking a random sample of opinions about a political question will not ask only committed part workers.

The size of the sample is important too. Some types of statistical analysis can be valid—that is fair and accurate—when done with a small sample, others cannot. Sometimes it is necessary to have a structure—that is a planned and organized sample and not a random one. All good statistical reports always explain very clearly what sampling methods were used.

After data are collected, they are processed. How this is done will depend on how the completed statistics or reports will be used. Sometimes data are just tabulated, that means added up and presented in lists under useful headings. Sometimes the statisticians make table that correlate lists of figures. This is the way to show mathematically how one group of figures is related to another. The most interesting thing that may be done with the figures is to use them as a basis for a prediction of what is likely to happen.

Statisticians base their predictions on the laws of probability. There are two kinds of probability, theoretical—which is worked out purely by mathematics—and empirical, which is the result of observation and experiment. Many research problems have to use both kinds of calculation. Engineers building a new bridge for example will use calculations of theoretical probability when they check things like the safety of the design. Results of observation and experiment will give the figures for empirical probability when they are checking the strength of the metals they will use.

You may wonder why, if statistics are so mathematical and scientific you often hear people saying that the opinion polls were wrong or the market research was a disaster. Both opinion polls and market research use statistics for their forecasts. When these fields produce poor and inaccurate statistics it usually is because the data collection was not very good. Opinion polls and market research rely on asking people questions. Planning the questions is not yet an exact science. Even a brilliant statistician will produce nonsense from poor data.

Probability

For one moment when a coin is tossed into the air it assumes a state of unpredictability. No one can say which face will come up. Yet toss that coin a lakh times and it will, with increasingly minor variations, came up heads half the time and tails the rest. In essence, this is the basis of the theory of probability—a branch of mathematics which deals with likelihoods, predictabilities and chance. First enunciated 300 years ago, probability's earliest applications were in the field of gambling, to which it still has very strong ties. But probability like its handmaiden and statistics have become an indispensable modem tool, predicting everything from life experiences to the positions of electrons. The Frenchman Pierre Simon de Laplace, pre-eminent in the field of probability, called it a science which began with play but evolved into the most important object of human knowledge.

Despite high stakes, early gamblers played with little idea of the percentages for or against them. No adequate mathematical analysis of gambling was made until 1654, when two French mathematicians, Pierre de Fermat and Blaise Pascal, in a long exchange of letters, laid the foundations of probability theory. For the first time the vagaries of games of chance could be reduced to that measurable percentage of certainty, the odds.

The theory of probability deals only with the general—never the specific. For example, probability gives a player one chance in 38 of winning on any given roulette number—but it makes no guarantee. He may win 10 times in a row; he may play 100 times and never win.

Besides refusing to be specific, probability is oblivious to setbacks. In a play with dice (36 pairs), a graphic display of what is possible with a single toss of two dice, shows that the chances of throwing snake eyes (double 1) are 1 in 36. But if a player should get snake eyes 100 times in a row, that would not lessen by one iota the 1 in 36 probability that his 101st turn will come up as a double 1. In this regard, probability has been likened to a kind of faith—unprovable on the one hand, immutable on the other.

Probability and its helpmate statistics are, in a sense, like two people approaching the same point from opposite ends of the lane. In probability the contributing factors are known, but a likely result can only be predicted. In statistics the end product is known but the causes are in doubt.

A knowledge of mathematics is not only desirable, it is essential in an increasingly technological world. Mathematics offers the reader a solid, scientific introduction to the subject, with emphasis placed on relevance of mathematics to modern life.

THE RESEARCH PROBLEM

The problem chosen for the present study is "Achievement in Mathematics at Intermediate (+2) level"

Why This Study !

Academic achievement is of paramount importance in the present socio-economic and cultural contexts. Obviously, at +2 stage, great emphasis is placed on achievement right from the beginning. This stage has its own systematic hierarchy which is largely based on achievement as this stage is a channel to enter professional course. So, the colleges tend to emphasize achievement with facilitates, among other things, to become professionals. The colleges perform the function of selection and differentiation among students on the basis of their scholastic and other attainments and open out avenues for advancement, again primarily in terms of achievement. A considerable number of students from +2 stage studying in colleges also go to other institutions of higher learning, such as law, general science courses, arts and commerce.

The effectiveness of any educational system is gauged to the extent the students involved in the system achieve, whether it be in cognitive, conative or psychomotor domain. In general terms, achievement refers to the scholastic or academic achievement of the student at the end of an educational programme. To maximize the achievement within a given set-up is, therefore, the goal of every educationist. Research has come out our aid by looking into what variables—personal, home, college, teacher. etc.,—promote achievement and what are deterrents to it. It has been thus indicated that a good number of variables, such as personality characteristics of the learners, the socio-economic status from which they hail, the educational aspirations, the organizational climate of the institution, etc. to mention a few, influence achievement in varying degrees

A lot of importance is given to the colleges because that is where the student spends these two vital years of intermediate course, and where he makes his future career. But, unfortunately, the situation in ordinary colleges, other than residential colleges, is not in any way encouraging. Innumerable maladies plague these temples of learning. The major problem in such colleges is regarding regularity. In many colleges, the studies, now-a-days, are interrupted by strikes, dharnas, bundhs, boycotts and so on resorted to one day by the students, another day by the teachers and on some other day by the non-teaching staff. With such frequent interruptions, the actual teaching period is going down drastically. Further, the concentration of the student is diverted by these disturbances.

It is also very important, in any competitive examination, that the student faces uniformly well in all subjects. Even if the student fares badly in one subject, the whole effort becomes waste. Now-a-days, a good combination of teachers is becoming a rarity in any college, because the cream of the educated youth, by the large, choose alternative vocations where they can make more money and consequently talented and efficient teachers have become a rare commodity. In many reputed colleges some of the teachers are outstanding where as others are mediocre, with the result the student fare very well in some subjects and only on an average scale and even very badly in others. So, there should be a perfect combination of teachers to impart uniformly good teaching in all subjects.

One more aspect in the place of Intermediate education is parents. Most of the parents are busy with their own occupations and are unable to devote enough time towards their children's education. They have the inclination but no time to do it. As a result, most of them resort to sending their children to tuitions and thing that their responsibility is over. They fail to supervise their studies and fail to help them when they are lagging behind in some subject or other. To comfort such parents, there is the necessity of an institute which can provide good and well coordinated supervision for their children's studies. For such an effective supervision, the inclination on the part of the teacher and an attachment between the teacher and the taught are the necessary pre-requisites.

Further, the students of Intermediate course studying in colleges just enter the adolescent stage, which is a stage of stress and storm. In this period, they must be properly guided and counselled, otherwise there arises the problem of maladjustment. If the adolescents are once properly guided and aroused right educational aspirations, they will excel in all aspects of life and education.

Governments have been spending crores on +2 or Intermediate education. But the results are not in proportion to the expenditure incurred. Only nearly 35 to 40 percent of the students are successful, this too from the contribution of private colleges. In other words, two thirds of the educational expenditure is squandered away for nothing.

To solve the above discussed maladies of Intermediate education, a new system of education relevant to the contemporary needs of the society came into lime light with a name called 'residential' college. Here one can see the perfect combination of talented teachers, a 24-hour supervision with a personal touch and involvement, suitable guidance and counselling, right educational aspirations in students, healthy competition among the students, alongwith a perfect supervision and administration of administrators.

Even admission into these residential colleges will be made mainly on merit basis and some private residential colleges keep in mind— an average student among meritorious students will be demoralized and will fare very badly even in future. Such a minute concepts also creeps into the minds of the administrators of the residential colleges.

The above arguments in favour of residential colleges and against non-residential colleges indicate that there should be a difference in the achievement of students studying in both kinds of these colleges. This study hence wants to identify the level of difference in the mathematics achievement of Intermediate students studying in residential and non-residential colleges.

The results of this study will help the educational planners, teachers and students to modify the present state of affairs as many students fail in Intermediate.

Objectives

The objectives of this research are —

1. To find out the level of achievement in mathematics of Intermediate students.
2. To compare the achievement in Mathematics of Intermediate students studying in residential and non-residential colleges..
3. To compare the achievement in mathematics of boys and girls.

Scope and Limitations

Mathematics at Intermediate level paves way to get admission into professional colleges such as Engineering, Technology, etc. As it decides the future vocations of +2 students, it is aimed to study the achievement only in mathematics. Importance was given to type of a college and sex. Locality, medium of instruction, management of colleges, infra-structural facilities, etc. have not been considered due to time factor. Influence of psycho-social variables on mathematics achievement have also not been taken into consideration.

Related Literature

Any worthwhile research study in any field of knowledge requires an adequate familiarity with the work which has already been done in the same area. A summary of the writings of recognized authorities and of previous research provides evidence that the research is familiar with what is already known and what is still unknown and untested. Since effective research is based upon past knowledge, this step helps to eliminate the duplication of what has been done, and provides useful hypotheses and helpful suggestions for significant investigation (Best, 1982).

Citing studies that show substantial agreement and those that seem to present conflicting conclusion help to sharpen and define understanding of existing knowledge in the problem area, provides a background for the research project, and makes the investigators aware of the status of the issue. Parading a long list of annotated studies relating to the problem is ineffective and inappropriate. Only those studies that are plainly relevant, competently executed and clearly reported should be included.

In searching related literature, the researchers should note certain important elements. They include—(1) Report of closely related studies that have been investigated, (2) Design of the study, including procedures employed and data-gathering instruments used, (3) Populations that were sampled and sampling method employed, (4) variables that were defined, (5) extraneous variables that could have affected the findings, (6) Faults that could have been avoided, and (7) Recommendations for further research.

The search for related literature is a time consuming process, even though it is necessary, as earlier stated, for a good research work. Hence this chapter is meant for the study of achievement and educational aspirations.

Education plays a vital role in building a society. A modern society cannot achieve its aims of economic growth, technical development and cultural advancement without fully harnessing the talents of its citizens. Educationists thus strive to develop fully the intellectual potential of the students and make efforts to see that their potentialities are fully realized and channelized for the benefit of the individuals and that of the society.

Educational opportunities, though open to all, do not seem to engage to any reasonable extent the capacities of those who seek to avail themselves of them. An eternal question baffling parents, educators and national planners is : Why do students of demonstrated ability flop in their academic efforts at school or college examinations? Academic under-achievement, more than academic failure, constitutes a grave problem as it amounts to wastage of human resources which is constructed as an irreparable loss to the society, which a developing country like ours can ill afford. This stimulated a number of researchers to undertake studies, like the present study, on factors influencing achievement.

The concepts of over-achievement and under-achievement, logically speaking are meaningful in relation of some expected level of performance. Theoretically, if one's performance is superior to the expected standard of performance then he may be regarded as over-achiever, whereas when one's performance is inferior then he may be regarded as under-achiever.

Scientists like Stanley, Ross, Frumar and Frazen felt that the phenomenon on over-achievement is, logically, spurious and meaningless since, according to them, no one can operate above the level of one's potential ability, from which most often, the standard of expected performance is derived. However, they assert that under-achievement is the indication level of full expression of one's potential ability..On accepting the theoretical definition of the concept of under-achievement which stresses that under-achievement is meaningful in relation to one's actual performance may be adjudged, we are justified to ask as to form which level the expected performance comes.

Broadly speaking, there are two ways open for answering the question regarding standard of expected performance. Either, the standard of expected performance may be subjective, or it may be objective. The subjective standard of expected performance may further be classified into two categories. In one type of the subjective standard of expected performance, the individual himself determines the standard of performance, whereas in the second type of subjective standard, the expected standard of performance is stipulated by the person who is operating as a 'significant - other' (parent or teacher) in one's process of socialization. We all know that the subjective standard of performance determined by significant others are so much subjective and irrational that they are rarely attainable. How-so-ever hard a student may try it is not possible to satisfy one's parents or teachers through his achievement.

Psychologically speaking, the subjective standard of expected performance, irrespective of the fact, whether it is arising from within or it is imposed by the parents or teachers from outside, is representing man's hopes and aspirations which are endless.

One more type of the subjective standard of expected performance is representing aspirations and hopes of one's spiritual leader or hero. Such a standard of expected performance is most often unrealized and may be termed as the ideal standard of expected performance.

The expected standard of performance which comes from within the individual, is the outcome of his own aspirations and satisfactions related to his achievements. Previous experiences of success result in guiding a person for raising his level of expectation. Some individuals may be satisfied with the previous achievement while others may want to settle for higher grades. They are often eager to learn more, confident to do it and ambitious to achieve more.

Taylor (1964) states that the value the student places upon his own worth effects his academic achievement. Very low level of expectation tends to make a pupil accept very low standard of achievement, very high expectations lead to discouragement. and diminished effort because he feels he cannot live upto what is required of him. To be practical, the level of expectation needs to be geared to suit each individual capability.

Many changes are being witnessed in organization, curricular, teaching strategies, etc. It is pertinent to seek systematic and up-to-date information on the significant correlates of a student achievement. It is also appropriate, in this context, to consider factors affecting the academic achievement such as the student's socio-economic background, educational aspirations, adjustment, etc. These factors are of almost theoretical and practical important in developing curricula and designing educational programmes to suit the needs of students with varied backgrounds. Further, the study of these factors assumes special significance in view of their implications in respect of day-to-day curriculum planning on the part of the classroom teachers. Studies on the correlates of achievement, thus, need to be thoroughly examined with a view to derive maximum benefit from their findings for the improvement of curricular development, efficient teaching, and better academic achievement.

Bhaskara Rao (1989) found an average achievement in secondary school pupils, Rathaiah (1992) found a high achievement in Intermediate students. Both of these studies identified a high achievement in residential students.

Sumangala and Malini (1993) identified the influence of mastery learning strategy on achievement in mathematics of secondary school level.

Bhaskara Rao and Pushpalatha (1994) didn't find any difference in the achievement of boys and girls. Rathaiah and Bhaskara Rao (1994) also found no difference in the achievement of boys and girls. But, Thakur (1972) and second International Science Study (1988) identified the superiority of boys in science achievement.

Research Design

Design is the heart of any research. For the present study the following aspects have been discussed which are concerned with the design of the study. Research procedures included the operational definitions of different terms used, the hypotheses that are framed for testing and the rational of the formulated hypotheses. Selection of he sample included the sampling techniques used, the reasons for the selection of a particular sampling technique, and the selection of the sample according to variables. Selection of tools included the selection of suitable tools for collection of data and the procedure followed to collect the data required for the study.

Before going into the details of the sample, sampling techniques, variables, hypotheses and tools, it will be worthwhile if we discuss the operational definitions of the key terms used in the study which will enlighten the characteristics involved in each term.

OPERATIONAL DEFINITIONS

The operational definitions of the important terms used in the study are defined and discussed hereby.

Mathematics

Mathematics has many branches. They may differ in the type of problems involved and in the practical application of their results. However mathematicians working in different branches often use many of the same basic concepts and operations.

Arithmetic includes the study of whole numbers, fractions and decimals, and operations of addition, subtraction, multiplication and division. It forms the foundation for other kinds of mathematics by providing such basic skills as counting and grouping objects, and measuring and comparing quantities.

Unlike arithmetic, algebra is not limited to work with specific numbers. Algebra involves solving problems with equations in which letters such as X and Y stand for unknown quantities. Algebra operation also use negative numbers and imaginary numbers.

Geometry is concerned with the properties and relationship of figures. Plane geometry deals with squares, circles and other figures that lie on a plane. Solid geometry involves such figures as cubes and spheres which have three dimensions.

Analytic geometry relates algebra and geometry. It provides a way to represent an algebraic equation as a line or curve on a graph. It makes it possible to write equations that exactly describe many curves.

Trigonometry is used widely by astronomers, navigators and surveyors to calculate angles distances when direct measurement is impossible. It deals with the relation between the sides and the angles of triangles. Certain relations between the length of sides of right angles are called trigonometric ratios. Using trigonometric ratios, a person can calculate the unknown angles and lengths. Formulas involving trigonometric ratios describe curves that physicists and engineers use to analyze the behaviour of heat, light, sound and other natural phenomena.

Calculus provides a way of solving many problems that involve motion of charging quantities. Differential calculus seeks to determine the rate at which a varying quantity charges. It is used to calculate the slope of a curve and the changing speed of a bullet. Integral calculus tries to find a quantity when the rate at which it is charging is known. It is used to calculate the area of a curved figure of the amount of work done by a varying force.

Analysis involves various mathematical operations with infinite quantities. It includes the study of infinite series, sequences of numbers of algebraic expressions that go on indefinitely. The concept of infinite series has important applications in such areas as the study of heat and of vibrating strings.

Probability is the mathematical study of the likelihood of events. It is used to determine the chances that an uncertain event may occur.

Statistics is the branch of mathematics concerned with the collection and analysis of large bodies of data to identify trends and over-all patterns. statistics relies heavily on probability. Statistical methods provide information to government, business and science.

Set theory deals with the nature and relations of sets. A set is a collection of items which may be numbers, ideas or objects. The study of sets is important in investigating. The most basic mathematical concepts.

In the field of logic, the branch of philosophy that deals with the rules of correct reasoning, mathematicians have developed symbolic logic. Symbolic logic is a formal system of reasoning that uses mathematical symbols and methods. Mathematicians have devised various systems of symbolic logic that have been important in the development of computers.

Achievement

Achievement in an educational institution may be taken to mean any desirable learning that is observed in the student. Since the word desirable implies a value judgement, it is obvious that a particular learning may be referred to as achievement or otherwise depending on whether it is considered desirable or not. Understood in this way, any behaviour that is learned may come within the scope of achievement. Achievement, according to Smith (1969), and Spencer and Helmrich (1983), is the task-oriented behaviour that allows the individual's performance to be evaluated according to some internally or externally imposed criterion, that involves the individual in competing with others or that otherwise involves some standard of excellence (Morgn, et. al. !986).

There is no gain·saying the fact that learning is not limited to mere acquisition of information, it also includes attitudes, interests, values, etc. Modern personality characteristics of the individual are learned. Therefore, the acquisition of desirable characteristics is as much an achievement as is knowledge of the principles of science or facts, world history or language and literature. Although achievement is used in this broad sense it is customary for schools and colleges to be concerned to a great extent with the development of knowledge, understanding and acquisition of skills (Narayana Rao, 1980). This may be in part owing to the fact that in the intellectual field the teacher can be relatively more certain of achieving the objectives he had set for himself than in other areas or domains.

Academic achievement is related to the acquisition of principles and generalizations and the capacity to perform efficiently, certain manipulations of objects, symbols and ideals. Assessment of academic performance has been largely confined to the evaluation in terms of information, knowledge and understanding. It is universally accepted that the acquisition of factual data is not an end in itself but an individual who has received education should show evidence of having understood them. But, for obvious reasons the examinations are largely confined to the measurement of the amount of information which students have acquired.

Achievement in terms of subject matter is conventionally assessed in our institutions by employing a system of marks or grades. It has been strongly argued that marks are necessary for effective teaching learning. Trabue (1926) felt that for classification, guidance and evidence of effort, marks are necessary. A committee of Principles of California listed the purposes of marks as the indication of the degree of mastery of subject matter and the prediction of future success. Madgen (1930) points out that marks set goals and motivate the students. Symons (1927) listed among the purposes of marks incitement of study, promotion of competitions, determination of promotion, assistance in education and vocational guidance, awarding credits and honors. It is universally accepted that marks serve for the basis of classification and certification, motivation and measurement of educational performance.

Achievement Test

Freeman (1965) defines a test of educational achievement as a test designed to measure knowledge, understanding, skills in a specified subject or group of subjects. Thus according to him, an educational achievement test measures an individual's knowledge and understanding or skills in a particular branch of knowledge. Further, Freeman is of the view that through educational achievement test, it is possible to ascertain how much does a person know after receiving education or training in a particular branch of knowledge. The standardized achievement tests are used to determine the degree of achievement in a specific subject matter (Smith, Krouse and Athkinson, 1969). Achievement test (Best, 1982) attempts to measure what an individuals has learned - his or her present level of performance.

An achievement test is also used for purposes of guidance and counselling. It has found useful in remedial teaching programmes as well as in determining the class to which a student should be admitted into. Administration of these tests at regular intervals is helpful to the teachers in knowing the kinds of difficulties faced by the pupils in learning. Finally, it may be stated that the achievement test may be used as an aid in the evaluation of teaching, the importance of instructional techniques, and the revision of curriculum content.

Residential Colleges

In the residential colleges, students stay on the college campus with their teachers instead of coming daily from their houses. So, they spend all their time either on the college premises or in the hostels. and pursue studies under the constant supervision of teachers. Such colleges of intermediate or +2 level are considered residential junior colleges.

Non-Residential Colleges

The students of these colleges will only be in the college campus during instructional hours and spend their remaining time at home or at other places. Such colleges are considered non-residential colleges.

Variables

A necessary requisite for any worthwhile research for the purpose of comparison. For the present study, the variables formulated are-residential versus non-residential colleges, and boys versus girls. The rationale for selecting the variables is discussed hereby.

Residential versus Non-Residential Colleges

Education has become indispensable for every one. The machinery of government is inadequate to educate all. According to earlier targets, we had to educate all children by the time they attain 14 years of age and the year 1960 was thought of as the year of fulfilling the target. Even though three decades have elapsed, we managed only to educate half of the total population. Here, one must not forget that private schools and colleges have the lion's share in promoting the education.

On the old Indian educational scenario, the gurukulas (Residential places of learning) played a very prominent role in educating the pupils or disciples. Later on, this system failed to cape with the changes that occurred in the society and disappeared almost to say frankly, and a new set-up of educational institutions came into existence and took deep roots. With the new system introduced and implemented by the British, many people got educated and obtained proficiency and efficiency in many fields of education and vocation.

Though the formal system of educational set-up has been providing education at its best to its non-boarders, it has certain disadvantages which include -poor teacher taught relationship, improper discipline, poor achievement, irrelevant teaching and learning strategies, less teacher pupil interaction, and so on. At this hour, the importance of residential system offered by the 'gurukulas' in good olden days is identified as the best system to solve many problems in educating a child and to provide quality education through better teaching learning strategies. This thought gave rise to many residential schools and colleges. The residential schools such as Andhra Pradesh Residential Schools, Andhra Pradesh Social Welfare Residential Schools, Jawahar Navodaya Schools, and colleges such as Andhra Pradesh Residential Junior Colleges, Andhra Pradesh Residential Degree Colleges, etc., have been established by both state government and central government. The residential institutions in Andhra Pradesh excelled in academic achievement and allied areas and proved worthy.

On seeing the performance of the students of A.P. Residential junior colleges established in Andhra Pradesh in the early 1980s by the Government of Andhra Pradesh, the private managements started establishing residential junior colleges, and at present they out number the non-residential colleges - both government and private- in volume and strength.

The Government of Andhra Pradesh, for example, has been spending to the tune of Rs. 200 crores on Intermediate education. The results are not in proportion to the expenditure incurred. Only 40 percent of the students pass. In other words two third of its expenditure is squandered away for nothing. When private educational institutions as are compared with those run by the government, the former are far better than the later in respect of physical facilities, administration and staff. Above all, they excel in the matter of results.

Now, private residential colleges have come up. They have been welcomed by those who want admission into professional courses. In fact, they have been weaning away a large number of students from government colleges. The Government institutions and government aided private colleges have been unable to attract the cream of Intermediate students. What are the features of residential system that have been attractive to students? Several other questions arise when we discuss the problem in detail.

Is the failure of government aided private and government colleges a factor in the success of private residential college system? Is the quality of teaching superior in private residential colleges to that of government and aided colleges? Whether laboratory and other necessary physical facilities contribute to their success? Is it the main aim of private residential system to earn more and more money? Are these colleges getting good results because of malpractices? Is there any real need for this rapid growth of residential colleges? Are these colleges a burden to the government or to the society?

Many think that the fast expansion of private colleges reflect the failure of the government in providing educational facilities to its people. But the education should not be monopolized by the Government. Such monopoly involves colossal financial expenditure which is not proportionately matched by results. Even in the most advanced countries government will not undertake the entire responsibility of educating its public.

When the private residential colleges grow, a large number of people who can afford to spend on education opt for private colleges and those who can't go to government institutions. With this the government can disburden itself, for most of the financially sound students get their education without compelling the government to spend anything on them. Then, there will also be a healthy competition between the two. so, privatisation of education brings healthy competition between the government and the private, reduces the pressure on government institutions and offers chances to the students who can afford to have such education.

Time is precious and the two year as student spend in his Intermediate course is more precious than any other period because that decides his future fate. In non-residential, government and aided colleges, teachers and students stay together for only five to six hours a day. The rest of the 18 to 19 hours, the student is left to his free will. Even if he wished to clear his doubts, teachers are not available. With the result the influence of society is greater on him than on his counterpart in residential colleges.

A student, on the other hand, is given ample opportunity in residential colleges to pursue his education with single-minded devotion and undivided attention, as the teachers are always available at hand. As the calibre of the students is very high, the teachers will also always be on the alert. As both teachers and students are committed to a goal and are led on the track of well-organized schedules, there is no room for diversion either for the student or for the teacher. This is evident from the wonderful results they produce. Unprecedented rush to these private residential colleges is an illustrative proof of their good performance. The colleges speak for themselves by their results.

In respect of facilities—buildings, hostels, laboratories, play fields—the private residential colleges score points against the government managed or aided colleges. Teaching, learning, playing and extra- curricular activities are all in a single campus. They are not touched by the ripples and waves of academic restlessness of other colleges. They are the real isolated islands of learning.

Students at the Intermediate level pass through adolescence, and they need careful handling as they pass through physiological and psychological changes with their attendant problems. The parents and the society are too busy to spare time to solve their problems. The teachers of government managed or aided colleges are deeply absorbed with their organizational problems. The residential colleges are started for this specific purpose of attending to the needs of Intermediate students. As the teachers, students and authorities are under one roof, any problem can be easily solved giving no room for dissatisfaction.

The residential colleges have been attracting students from all over the State. So the students are given a wonderful opportunity to mingle and develop their personalities. These colleges forge emotional integration also among the students. While other colleges are the victims of local and non-local restraints, these residential colleges fully represent the culture of the state.

Finally, with these advantages, the residential system or the old gurukula system which we gave up long ago has come to stay. Residential colleges, may overcome the maladies that afflict the academic world to certain extent.

Considering the above facts, the students of residential and non-residential colleges were taken into consideration to study the achievement in mathematics of the students.

Boys Versus Girls

In olden days, boys were educated and the girls were restricted to their kitchens by their adult community. Times changed and the adults recognized the importance of women education. In the words of our former Prime Minister Pandit Jawharlal Nehru, "if you educate a man you educate only one person, if you educate a woman you educate the entire family". In due course, women education gained importance and many parents are encouraging their daughters to pursue higher education. Women are also showing excellence in all fields and their presence is felt almost in all areas of knowledge.

As the psychological conditions, exposure to society, education and other aspects of girls and boys vary differently, there may be significant difference in the performance. The boys may be exposed to the society to a larger extent, but the girls spend most of their time in going through books or helping their parents at home. These factors will show their influence on their mental development and performance.

Under these circumstances, the variable sex has been selected to identify its sole on achievement in mathematics.

HYPOTHESES

Mathematics has become an important aspect of human life and has occupied and kept this important place from the earliest times and is perhaps the only subject which merits this distinction. That is why the education commission-1964-66 observed that "we cannot overstress the importance of mathematics in relation to science, education and research. This has always been so, but at no time has the significance of mathematics been greater than today...... it is important that deliberate effort is made to place India on the 'world map of Mathematics' within the next two decades or so". Of course, we are the pioneers of numerals as well we are the leaders of many mathematical areas throughout the ages.

Mathematics has played a decisive role in building up our civilizations. But in doing so, it has also made itself essential for the existence and progress of modern world. In modern world we have to be more and more exact, hence mathematics is very important for a common man. In the age of rates, taxes, insurance, premia, savings, interests, rents, dividends, percentages, etc., only a person with mathematical background can be reasonably sure that he is getting his due in the society.

Such an important subject has been made a compulsory subject at school level and an elective at higher levels of learning. We can only identify the understanding and use of mathematics if we measure the achievement of the pursuers of mathematics.

Hypothesis 1.

The achievement of Intermediate students in mathematics will be high.

Hypothesis 2.

There will be a significant difference in the level of achievement in mathematics of Intermediate students studying in residential and non-residential colleges.

Hypothesis 3.

There will be a significant difference in the achievement in mathematics of boys and girls.

SAMPLE

After finalizing the objectives of the present study, consideration was given to whether the entire population is to be made the subject for data collection or a particular group is to be selected as representative of the whole population. The 'entire population' here refers to all the Intermediate course students.

Of the above two techniques, the selection of a group as a representative of the whole population was found to be more convenient and suitable. This techniques leads to a considerable saving of time, effort and finance. The numbers of students selected will be small, and so it is possible to make accurate and reliable results. As this sampling technique has many advantages, it was selected for the collection of data.

In any social research, various methods are utilized for selection and drawing of samples. After a detailed study of all these methods, and considering the variables selected from the research work, the *stratified sampling method* was found to be most suitable.

In the stratified sampling method, the entire population is divided into small homogeneous groups or strata, and then a sample is selected within each group. Every sampling unit in the population is placed in one of the strata prior to the selection of the sample so that the sum of the strata is identical with the population.

Stratified sampling method has certain merits and advantages as a technique of sampling. Auckoff has rightly said that 'stratified sampling enables the researcher to make a comparison of properties of the strata as well as to estimate population characteristics.

In this stratified sampling method, the investigator has greater control over the selection of the sample when compared with random sampling. In random sampling, although every group has a chance of being selected and included in the sample, there is every possibility, and sometimes it does happen, that certain important groups are left unrepresented. But in stratified sampling method no important group is likely to be left out.

Stratified sampling method is the ideal one when comparison between different variables has to be made. For example, if comparison has to be made between boys and girls, it would be very difficult to select the required number of units through any other method of sampling. If any other method is used, the problem of bias and prejudice creeps in.

Replacement of units is also possible in the stratified sampling method. Normally if a particular unit is not accessible for a study, it is difficult to replace it by another, but in this method it is possible. Stephen states that 'stratification automatically brings about a replacement of persons lost to the sample, by persons of the same stratum, thus partly correcting the basis that would result if there were no replacement of loses'. As the entire population is divided into particular strata it is easy and convenient to replace an inaccessible case by an accessible one.

In stratified sampling method, much depends on stratification process. The following precautions were taken while stratifying the population: the variables involved in the study were taken note of; care was taken to see that each stratum in the universe was large enough in size so that selection of items could be done on random basis; the strata formed were definite and clear cut; each stratum was free from influence of the other; that there was no overlapping.

Before actually selecting the sample, certain fundamental principles were considered to make the sample scientific and clear-cut.

Firstly, the 'universe' was clearly defined. In the technical phraseology of research, the whole population out of which the samples are selected is known as the 'universe'. For the present research work, the universe includes all the students of Intermediate studying in Andhra Pradesh. The study was limited to a particular geographical area, viz., Guntur district, to facilitate appropriate sample selection and to avoid bias and prejudice.

Secondly, decision has to be made about the units of the sample. A unit of sample may be a house, a family, a group of individuals or a single individual. A good unit should possess the following characteristics.

1. *Clarity:* The unit should be clearly defined in unambiguous terms. This would make the study easy and efficient. For the present research work, a sampling unit is defined as student of Intermediate studying in any college;

2. *Suitability :* A good unit should be well suited to the problem under study. Since the problem is the possession and comparison of achievement in mathematics of Intermediate students, the unit selected is well suited to the problem;

3. *Accessibility:* The unit selected should be easily accessible to the researchers. If the units selected are difficult to reach and if they fail to make use of them, the study would be vitiated. The selected sampling unit, *i.e.*, a Intermediate students easily accessible since he/she could be approached in any college.

The third principle to be considered while selecting a sample is the availability and preparation of the source list. This is an important factor that makes representative selection possible. A source list is the list which contains the names of the units of the universe from which the sample may be selected. It may exist even before the beginning of the project or it may be prepared afresh by the investigators themselves. Without a source list, study through the sampling method is no possible. For the present research work, a source list, consisting of the names of colleges is used. Care was taken to see that the source list was up-to-date and valid and that there was no repetition of names of the colleges. This source list was found to be relevant and suitable because it included all the colleges as the study deals with the Intermediate students.

Besides considering these principles, it is extremely important to think about the size of the sample to be selected. If the sample is either too small or too large, it will make the study difficult and also make the results untenable. According to Parten, 'an optimum sample in survey is one which fulfils the requirements of effective representativeness, reliability and flexibility. The sample should be small enough to avoid intolerable sampling error. The size of sample for the present research work was decided after considering the following factors.

Since an intensive study was planned, a very large number of samples is not selected. In case of an intensive study very large number of samples is not so useful as it involve huge consumption of the resources. Hence, a smaller sample is found to be convenient.

The size and selection of the samples are also influenced by the nature of the universe. If the universe is homogeneous, even a small-sized sample may yield dependable and required results. If the universe is heterogeneous, small-sized samples may not be useful. In case of the present study, the heterogeneous universe was split into smaller homogeneous strata or groups and the samples were selected from these strata. For example, all the Intermediate students were broadly grouped under residential and non-residential students. A sample was selected from each of these two groups.

The researchers need to determine the number of the groups to be formed. In case the number of groups proposed in large, the size of the samples shall have to be large so that every group should be of proper size and suit the requirements of the study. In case the number of groups proposed is small, even small-sized samples can fulfil the requirement. In case of the present study, the universe was divided into girls and boys and residential and non-residential students. Since the number of groups were limited, a reasonable sample was selected from each of these groups.

Practical consideration and accuracy also play a vital role in determining the size of the sample. Every study is guided by certain practical considerations such as time, resources, accessibility of the data, etc. Generally, it is believed that a large-sized sample is more representative and usually produces accurate results. This, of course, depends upon the technique of sampling used. If the sampling technique is scientific, even small-sized samples can produce dependable and accurate results. While selecting the size of the sample for the present study, practical considerations like the availability of resources and time were taken into consideration. Care was taken to make the sample selection technique as scientific as possible.

The size of the sample is also governed by the size of the tools to be sued. In case the tools are short, and the questions asked pertain to certain limited factors, a large sample can be selected. In case the tools are large and the questions complicated, the sample should be small in size so that, from administrative point of view, the researchers may not be put to unnecessary troubles. In the present study, as the marks are only to be obtain the sample selected is reasonably large.

The sampling method also determines the size of the sample. When random sampling method is used, the samples have to be large. On the other hand if samples are selected through stratified sampling method, the reliability can be achieved even with the help of the small-sized samples.

Taking these factors into consideration which influence the size of the sample, it was decided that an ideal sample would consist of two hundred students. This sample is small enough to avoid unnecessary expenditure and large enough to avoid intolerable sampling errors.

After deciding about the sampling method and the size of the sample, the universe selected was divided into different strata. The variables chosen for the study were considered to divide the universe. The 2 variables chosen were : boys versus girls and residential versus non-residential colleges.

Taking the variable which compares residential and non-residential areas at first instance, the universe which geographically consisted of Guntur district was split into residential and non-residential colleges. An equal number of sample was taken from both types of colleges. Equal weightage was given to boys and girls in each of the colleges.

Table 1: Distribution of Sample

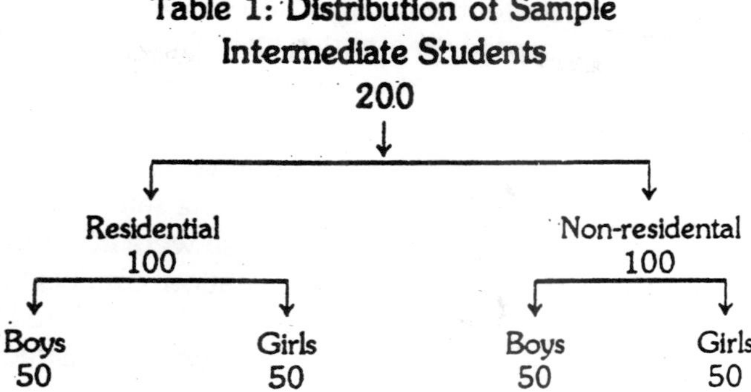

DATA COLLECTION

A research tool plays a major role in any worthwhile research, as it is the sole factor in determining the sound data and in arriving at perfect conclusions about the problem or study in hand, which, ultimately, helps in providing suitable remedial measures to the problem concerned.

The selection and use of tools can be done in two ways. The first one is to construct a tool independently by the researcher for his own study. Here, there are many problems in doing so. On construction of own tools, Anand and Padma feel that 'A note of caution has to be struck when a researcher develops a tool for his study by merely pooling some items and does not subject it to the sophisticated techniques of tool construction. The result would be then obvious, a poor quality research. With this, one can say that preparation and standardization of tools is a major task, and one should take care in aspects like selection of area and sample, pooling up of statements related to the area, consulting the experts, and application of sophisticated statistical techniques'.

The other way of selection and use of tools is right selection of tools from already standardized ones available in the field of study. Here also it involves a tedious job in locating the tools and identifying their usefulness to the study on hand. Even then, this technique is very useful when a research work is taken to study in depth and when the research work involves a good number of variables. Some people believe that some of the instruments available do not measure up to their standards. Hence new ones. In some instances, consideration should be given to the logistics of the situation. Lacking time and financial resources for the construction of a test, many researchers cannot expect to produce a better instrument. In these cases, the most logical procedure that he can follow is to choose the best instrument available for his purpose.

To measure the achievement in mathematics, marks of the Junior Intermediate Public Examinations of the sample were taken. These marks were considered became these were achieved by the sample from the common public examination conducted by the Board of Intermediate Education. Government of Andhra Pradesh, Hyderabad, it is being a testing organization established by the Government. Another factor contributed to consider these marks is that there are no standardized tests with the syllabus of the Government of Andhra Pradesh. As the investigation are interested in measuring the achievement of Intermediate Students, the marks obtained though a state-wide examination will serve the purpose.

Data Analysis

The organization, analysis and interpretation of data and formulation of conclusions and generalizations are necessary to get a meaningful picture out of the raw information collected. The analysis and interpretation of data involve the objective material in the possession of the researcher and his subjective reactions and desires to derive from the data the inherent meanings in their relation to the problem (Rummel 1, 1958).

The mass data collected through the use of various tools, need to be systematized and organized, i.e., edited, classified and tabulated before it can serve the purpose. Here, editing implied the checking of gathered data for accuracy, utility and completeness; classifying refers to the dividing of the information into recording of the classified material in accurate mathematical terms, analysis of data means studying the tabulated material in order to determine inherent facts or meanings. It involves breaking down the existing complex factors into simpler parts and putting the parts together in new arrangements for purposes of interpretation.

The mathematics marks of Junior Intermediate Public Examinations of each student were taken to find out the achievement status of total sample as well as each sub-sample. The maximum score that a student can get is 150 and the minimum is 1. In the present study, the highest score secured was 150 and the lowest score was 21.

For the purpose of classification of achievement into 3

categories, viz., low, average and high, the following procedure was followed. As the sample was selected only from Mathematics group the students scored very well. Hence the categorization was made as a student who scored below 74 was put in low achievement group, who secured between 75 to 104 was kept in average achievement group and who scored 105 and above was placed in high achievement group as per normal probability of distribution.

The mean scores were used to identify the achievement status of total sample and to compare the sub-sample variation. The values of standard deviation were used to measure the spread (dispersion) of scores in the distribution (Best). The critical ratios were calculated to test the significant difference in the means of the two sub-samples of each variable.

The chi-square (x^2) test of independence was applied for comparing the experimentally obtained results with those to be expected theoretically on some hypothesis (Garret, 1979)

HYPOTHESIS 1

The achievement of Intermediate Students in Mathematics will be high.

To test the validity of hypothesis -1, the total marks of all the samples were calculated to arrive at mean and standard deviation of the sample. The results are as follows.

Table 2: Achievement of the Whole Sample

Sample	*Sample Size*	*Mean*	*Standard Deviation*
Whole	200	98.7	31.8

It is clear, from the table -2, that the Intermediate mathematics students were high in achievement. But as per standard deviation, the dispersion of scores was high in the units of the sample.

The chi-square test of independence was applied to test the divergence of observed results from those expected theoretically.

As the chi-square test value was significant, the achievement of Intermediate students was not distributed normally. The achievement trend was tending towards high.

The hypothesis that "the achievement of Intermediate students will be high" can be accepted.

Table 3: Distribution of Achievement in the Whole Sample.

Sample Size		Low	Average	High	x^2
200	f_0	48	66	86	80.34*
	f_e	32	136	32	

* Significant at 0.01 level

f_0 = frequency of occurrence of observed or experimentally determined facts.

f_e = frequency of occurrence expected theoretically.

HYPOTHESIS 2

There will be a significant difference in the level of achievement in mathematics of Intermediate students studying in residential and non-residential colleges.

To compare the difference in the level of achievement in residential and non-residential college students, the following statistical treatment was given.

Table 4 : Comparison of Achievement of Residential and Non-Residential College Students

Variable	*Sample Size*	*Mean*	*S.D.*	*Mean Difference*	*Critical Ratio*
Residential	100	111.1	30.81	24.6	1.74*
Non-Residential	100	86.5	27.77		

* Significant at 0.01 level

It is clear, from the table 4, that there was a great significant difference in the level of achievement in the students studying in residential and non-residential colleges. The students of residential colleges were better in achievement than those of non-residential colleges.

As a great difference was seen in the level of achievement in the variables, the distribution of it was studied in both sub-samples.

The distribution of achievement was not normal in both the cases. The achievement concentration in residential colleges was in very high achievement group and it was very high in average achievement group in non-residential colleges.

Table 5: Distribution of Achievement in Residential and Non-Residential College Students

Variable	*Sample Size*		*Low*	*Average*	*High*	x^2
Residential	100	f_o	15	22	63	169.23*
		f_e	16	68	16	
Non-Residential	100	f_o	33	44	23	29.59*
		f_e	16	68	16	

* Significant at 0.01 level

The hypothesis that "there will be a significant difference in the level of achievement in mathematics of Intermediate students studying in residential and non-residential junior colleges" can be accepted.

HYPOTHESIS 3

There will be a significant difference in the level of achievement in mathematics of the boys and girls.

A comparison was made to identify the difference in the achievement of boys and girls. The data as follows.

Table 6: Comparison of Achievement of Boys and Girls.

Variable	*Sample Size*	*Mean*	*S.D.*	*Mean Difference*	*Critical Ratio*
Boys	100	102.1	31.196	18.6	1.42*
Girls	100	83.5	32.062		

* Significant at 0.01 level

According to the mean scores and critical ratio there was a difference in the achievement of boys and girls.

As there was difference in the achievement of boys and girls, it was tried to identify the distribution of achievement in both the sub-samples.

Table 7: Distribution of Achievement in Boys and Girls.

Variable	*Sample Size*		*Low*	*Average*	*High*	x^2
Boys	100	f_0	21	31	48	67.69*
		f_e	16	68	16	
Girls	100	f_0	25	36	39	59.182*
		f_e	16	68	16	

* Significant at 0.01 level

There was, as per the chi-square value, boys are slightly better in achievement.

The hypothesis that "there will be a significant difference in the level of achievement in mathematics of boys and girls" can be accepted.

Summary, Conclusions and Discussion

The work of mathematicians may be divided into pure mathematics and applied mathematics. Pure mathematics seeks to advance mathematical knowledge for its own sake rather than for any immediate practical use. For example, a mathematician may create a system of geometry for an imaginary world where objects have more dimensions than just length, width and depth. Applied mathematics seeks to develop mathematical techniques for use in science and other fields. The boundary between pure and applied mathematics is not clear. Ideas developed in pure mathematics often have practical applications and work in applied mathematics frequently leads to research in pure mathematics.

Nearly every part of our lives involve mathematics. It was played an essential role in the development of modern technology, tools, materials, techniques and sources of power that make our lives and work easier.

We use mathematics for such simple tasks as telling time from a clock or counting our change after making a purchase. We also use mathematics for such complex tasks as taking up a household budget or balancing our cheque book. Cooking, driving, gardening, sewing and many other common activities involve mathematical calculations. Mathematics is also a part of many games, hobbies and sports.

Mathematics is an essential part of nearly all scientific studies. It help scientists design experiments and analyze data. Scientists use mathematical formulas to express their findings precisely and to make predictions based on their findings. The physical sciences, such as astronomy, chemistry and physics rely heavily on mathematics. Such social sciences as economics, psychology and sociology also depend greatly on statistics and other kinds of mathematics.

Mathematics helps industries to design, develop and test products and manufacturing processes. Mathematics is necessary in designing bridges, buildings, dams, highways, tunnels and other architectural and engineering projects.

Mathematics is used in transactions that involve buying and selling. Business needs mathematics to keep records of such things as stock levels and employee's hours and wages. Bankers use mathematics to handle and invest funds. Mathematics helps insurance companies calculate risks and compute the rates charged for insurance coverage.

The subject mathematics has developed through ages. Prehistoric people probably first counted with their fingers. They also had various methods for recording such quantities as the number of animals in a herd or the days since the full moon. To represent such amounts, they used a corresponding number of pebbles, knots in a cord, or marks on wood, bone or stone. They also learned to use regular shapes when they moulded pottery or carved arrow heads.

By about 3000 B.C., mathematicians of ancient Egypt used a decimal system (a system of counting in groups of 10) without place value. The Egyptians pioneered in geometry, developing formulas for finding the area and volume of simple figures. Egyptian mathematics had many practical applications, ranging from surveying fields after the annual floods to making the intricate calculations necessary to build the pyramids.

By 2100 B.C., the people of ancient Babylonia had developed a 'sexadecimal system"- a system based on groups of 60. Today, we use such a system to measure time in hours, minutes and seconds. Historians do not know exactly how the Babylonian system developed. They think it may have arisen from the use of weights and measures based on groups of 60. This system had important uses in astronomy, and also in commerce, because 60 can be divided easily. The Babylonians went well beyond Egyptians in algebra and geometry.

Ancient Greek scholars became the first people to explore pure mathematics apart from practical problems. They made important advances by introducing the concepts of logical deduction and proof in order to create a systematic theory of mathematics. According to tradition, one of the first to provide mathematical proofs based on education was the philosopher Thales, who did his work in geometry about 600 B.C

The Greek philosopher Pythagoras, who lived about 550 B.C., explored the nature of numbers, believing that everything could be understood in terms of whole numbers or their ratios. However, about 400 B.C., the Greeks discovered 'irrational numbers' and they recognized that Pythagorean ideas were incomplete. About 370 B.C., Exdoxus of Cnidus, a Greek astronomer, formulated a theory of proportions to resolve problems associated with irrational numbers. He also developed the method of exhaustion, a way of determining areas of curved figures, which foreshadowed integral calculus.

Euclid, one of the foremost Greek mathematicians wrote the 'Elements' about 300 B.C. In this book, Euclid constructed an entire system of geometry by means of abstract definitions and logical deductions. During the 200 B.C., the Greek mathematician Archimedes extended the method of exhaustion. Using a 96-sided figure to approximate a circle, he calculated a highly accurate value of 'Pi' About A. D. 150, the Greek astronomer Ptolemy applied geometry and trigonometry to astronomy in a 13-part work on the motions of the planets. It became known as the 'Almagest' meaning the greatest.

The Romans showed little interest in pure mathematics. However, they applied mathematical principles in such fields as commerce, engineering and warfare.

Scholars in the Arab world translated and preserved the works of ancient Greek mathematicians and made their own original contributions as well. A book written about 825 A.D. by the Arab mathematician al-Khowarizmi described a numeration system developed in India. This decimal system, which used place values and zero, became known as the Hindu-Arabic numerical system. Al-

Khowarizmi also wrote an influential book about algebra. The word 'algebra' comes form the Arabic title of this book.

In the mid-1100s, a Latin translation of Al-Khowarizmi's book on arithmetic introduced the Hindu-Arabic numeral system to Europe. In 1202, Leonardo Fibonacci, and Italian mathematician, published a book on algebra that helped promote this system. Hindu-Arabic numerals gradually replaced Roman numerals in Europe.

Arab astronomers of the 900s, made major contributions to trigonometry. During the 1000s, an Arab physicist, Alhazen, applied geometry topics. The Persian poet and astronomer Omar Khayyam wrote an important book on algebra about 1100. In the 1200s, Nasir Eddin al-Tusi, a Persian mathematician, created ingenious mathematical models for use in astronomy.

During the 1400s and 1500s, European explorers sought new overseas trade routes, stimulating the application of mathematics to navigation and commerce. Mathematics also played a part in artistic creativity. Renaissance artists applied principles of geometry and created a system of linear perspective that gave their paintings an illusion of depth and distance. The invention of printing with movable type in the mid-1400s resulted in speedy and widespread communication of mathematical knowledge.

The Renaissance also brought major advances in pure mathematics. In a book published in 1533, a German mathematician known as Regiomontanus established trigonometry as a field separate from astronomy. French mathematician Francois viete made advances in algebra in a book published in 1591.

By 1600, the increased use of mathematics and the growth of the experimental method were contributing to revolutionary advances in knowledge. In 1543, Nicolus Copernicus, a Polish astronomer, published an influential book in which he argued that the sun, not the earth, is the centre of universe. His book sparked intense interest in mathematics and its applications, especially to the study of the motions of the earth and other heavenly bodies. In 1614, John Napier, a Scottish mathematician, published his discovery of logarithms, numbers that can be used to simplify such complicated calculations as those used in astronomy. Galileo, an Italian astronomer, found that many types of motion can be analyzed mathematically.

In a book published in 1637, french philosopher Rene Descartes proposed mathematics as the perfect model for reasoning. His invention of analytic geometry illustrated the exactness and certainty that mathematics can provide. Another French mathematician of the 1600s. Pierre de 'Fermat, founded modern number theory. He and french philosopher Blaise Pascal explored probability theory. Fermat's work helped lay a foundation for calculus.

The English scientist Isaac Newton invented calculus in the mid-1660s, He first mentioned his discovery in a book published in 1687. Working independently, the German philosopher and mathematician Gottfried Wilhelm Leibniz also invented Calculus in the mid- 1670s. He published his findings in 1684 and 1686.

A remarkable family of Swiss mathematicians, the Bernoullis, made many contributions to mathematics during the late 1600s and the 1700s. Jakob Bernoulli did pioneering work in analytic geometry and wrote about probability theory. Jakob's brother Johann also worked in analytic geometry and in mathematical astronomy and physics. Johann's son Nicolaus helped to advance probability theory. Johann's son Dainel used mathematics to study the motion of fluids and the properties of vibrating strings.

During the mid-1700s. Swiss mathematicians Leonhard Euler advanced in calculus by showing that the operations of differentiation and integration were opposites. Beginning in the late 1700s, French mathematician Joseph L. Lagrange worked to develop a firmer foundation for calculus. He was suspicious of relying on assumptions from geometry and instead developed calculus entirely in terms of algebra.

Public education expanded rapidly and mathematics became a standard part of university education. Many of the great works in mathematics of the 1800s were written as text books. In the 1790s and 1800s, French mathematician Adrien Marie Legendre wrote particularly influential text books and did work in calculus, geometry and number theory. Important calculus text books by French mathematician Augustin Louis Cauchy were published in the 1820s. Cauchy and Jean Baptiste Fourier, another French mathematician, made significant advances in mathematical physics.

Karl Friedrich Gauss. a German mathematician, proved the fundamental theorem of algebra which states that every equation has at-least one root. His work with imaginary numbers led to their increased acceptance. In the 1810s Gauss developed a non-Euclidean geometry but did not publish his discovery separately. Janos Bolyati of Hungary and Nikolai Lobachevsky of Russia also developed non-Euclidean geometries. They published their discoveries about 1830. In the mid-1800s, George Friedrich Riemann of Germany developed another non-Euclidean geometry.

During the early 1800s, the works of German mathematician august Fredinand Mobius helped develop a study in geometry that became known as topology. Topology explores the properties of geometrical figure that do not change when the figure is bent or stretched.

In the late 1800s, German mathematician Karl Theodor Weierstrass worked to establish a more solid theoretical foundation for calculus. In the 1870s and 1880s, his student George Cantor developed set theory and a mathematical theory of the infinite.

Much work in applied mathematics was performed in the 1800s. In Great Britain, Charles Babbage developed early mechanical computing machines and George Boote created a system of symbolic logic. During the late 1800s, French mathematician Jules Henri Poincare contributed to probability theory, celestial mechanics, topology and the study of electromagnetic waves.

Many mathematicians of the 1900s have shown concern for philosophical foundation of mathematics. In order to eliminate contradictions, some mathematicians have used logic to develop mathematics from a set of axioms, Two British philosophers and mathematicians, Alfred Whitehead and Bertrand Russell, promoted a philosophy of mathematics called logicism. In their three-volume work, Principia Mathematica (1910-1913), they argues that all propositions (Statements) in mathematics can be derived logically from just a few axioms, the statements considered to be true.

David Hilbert, a German mathematician of the early 1900s, was a formalist. Formalists consider mathematics to be a purely formal system of rules. Hilbert's work led to the study of imaginary spaces with a infinite number of dimensions.

Beginning in the early 1900s, Dutch mathematician Luitzen Brouwer championed intuitionism. He believed people understand the laws of mathematics by intuition the knowledge not gained by reasoning or experience.

In the early 1930s, Austrian mathematician Kurt Godel demonstrated that for any logical system there are always theorems that can't be proven either true or false by the axioms within that system. He found this to be true even of basic arithmetic.

Mathematicians have made major advances in the study of abstract mathematical structures during the 1990s. One such mathematical structure is the group. A group is a collection of items, which may be numbers, and rules for some operation with these items such as addition or multiplication. Group theory is useful in many areas of mathematics and such fields as subatomic physics.

Since 1939, a group of mathematicians, most of whom are French, have published an influential series of books under the pen name Nicolas Bourbani. This series takes and abstract approach to mathematics using axiom systems and set theory. New areas of mathematical specialization have arisen during the 1900s, including systems analysis and computer science. Advances in mathematical logic have been essential to the development of electronic computers. Computers, in turn, enabled mathematicians to complete long and complicated calculations quickly since 1970s. Computer-based mathematical models have became widely used to study weather patterns, economic relationships and many other systems.

Identifying the importance of mathematics, the present study has been taken up to assess the achievement of Intermediate students in mathematics.

The major objectives of this research are -1. To find out the achievement in mathematics of Intermediate students and 2. To compare the mathematics achievement of boys and girls and students of residential and non-residential colleges.

Considering their role in determining achievement in mathematics, variables namely residential college students versus non-residential college students and boys versus girls have been selected for this study.

The hypotheses framed fro the present research are —

1. The achievement of Intermediate students in mathematics will be high,
2. There will be a significant difference in the level of achievement in mathematics of Intermediate students studying in residential and non-residential colleges, and

3. There will be a significant difference in the achievement in mathematics of boys and girls.

Stratified sampling technique has been used to select the sample for data collection. Two hundred Intermediate students, one hundred each from residential and non-residential colleges, are selected. Equal weightage is given to boys and girls.

The marks secured by the sample in their Junior Intermediate Public Examinations in Mathematics are used for data analysis to draw conclusions for discussion.

The present study has resulted in drawing the following conclusions which anu be utilized in improving the present state of affairs in academic achievement.

The achievement of Intermediate students in Mathematics was high. The distribution of the achievement in Intermediate students was tending towards high achievement.

A limited number of independent studies are available on achievement at various levels of school education. But only one study is available particularly with the Intermediate students. Bhaskara Rao (1989) found that achievement in Biology was average in the secondary school pupils. Rani (1980) found that the academic achievement of under-graduate engineering S.C. students was significantly lower than that of non-S.C. students. The study of Aruna (1981) also reported similar results. The result of the present study is supporting the study of Rathaiah and Bhaskara Rao (1994).

The factors contributing to this high achievement are many and multi-dimensional. The samples selected were studying in the well-equipped colleges. The staff was experienced and the students of mathematics were known for their hard work aspiring high goals. And most important thing is there is a stiff competition between the residential and non-residential colleges about the admission of the students and, of course, about their survival also. If the achievement is not good in residential colleges they would not be self-sufficient in their maintenance. So, the administrators and the lecturers work efficiently with perfect co-ordination to get higher academic achievement through their clientele. To cope up with the residential colleges the staff of the non-residential colleges are also putting their students on heels. Besides this stiff competition between residential and non-residential colleges, availability of adequate laboratory and library facilities, conducive learning atmosphere, experience and efforts of teaching community, high educational aspirations of residential college students have also been contributed for this high achievement. If these conditions are provided in non-residential colleges also then there will be no question of chronic under-achievement and the students will also come out of the examinations with flying colours.

The achievement in residential and non-residential colleges was different. The students studying in residential colleges were with high achievement whereas those studying in non-residential colleges were with average achievement. The achievement distribution in the sub-sample was also different. The concentration of achievement in residential colleges was towards high achievement, but it was in average achievement group in non-residential colleges. The achievement trend was also tending towards high achievement in residential colleges and its trends was reverse in the case of non-residential colleges.

Bhaskara Rao (1989) and Rathaiah and Bhaskara Rao (1994) also found that the pupils of residential system were superior in achievement than their counterparts. The facilities that are available in residential colleges are not available in non-residential colleges. The residential colleges also select the cream of student community for them. The facilities such as good libraries, well furnished laboratories, appropriate teaching learning strategies, time-table of the institution, institutional set-up, study habits of the students, administrators' capacity, advantages of residential system, rapport between teacher and taught media, expertise and commitment of the teaching community, intelligence and hard work of the student clientele might have helped in achieving a high achievement by the residential college students. Srinivasa Rao and Subramanyam (1982) identified that among the school factors accommodation, educational level and experience of teachers, availability of instructional material, books and reading room facilities have influenced on reading attainment, which is one of the prime factors of achievement. So, the above facilities, as far as possible, should be extended to all non-residential colleges.

Boys and girls differed in achievement in mathematics. Boys scored highly but the girls secured an average achievement. The concentration of boys and girls was towards higher achievement.

The result of the present study is supporting the finding of Thakur (1972) and the Second International Science Study (1988) where the boys were superior to girls in science achievement. But Rathaiah and Bhaskara Rao (1994) found no significant difference in the level of achievement in boys and girls. As the boys are exposed to the society to a larger extent and as the needs of the boys are given top priority in the houses they might have got higher achievement. The reasons for an average achievement in girls may be due to home conditions and parents negative attitude towards women education. The parents, the society, and the educationists must give equal priority to both boys and girls as far as education is concerned.

Suggestions for Further Research

The present study proposes the following studies for future research.

1. This study can be extended to a large sample studying.
2. Comparative studies may be taken up to find out the variance in rural and urban students, and English and Telugu medium students.
3. Students may be taken up to identify the other socio-psycho correlates of achievement in mathematics.
4. Studies may be conducted on the role of audio visual teaching aids, laboratory and library facilities in enhancing the achievement in mathematics.
5. Studies may be carried out to find out the role of exhibitions, clubs, museums and other mathematical centres in promoting the achievement in mathematics.

Bibliography

Aggrawal, S.M. (1990). *A Course in Teaching of Modern Mathematics*. New Delhi : Dhanpat Rai & Sons.

Alphen, Moris L. (1946, October). "The Ability to Test Hypotheses". *Science Education*. 30 : 220-229.

Approach Paper on Science and Mathematics in General Education. Report of the working group on Science & Mathematics, September 1985. Department of Education in Science & Mathematics, National Council of Education Research and Training, New Delhi.

Atkinson, J. Myron and R. Will Burnell, "Science Education". *Enclyclopedia of Educational Research*, 4th ed. 1192-1205.

Best John W. (1982). *Research in Education*, 4th ed. New Delhi: Prentice Hall of India Pvt. Ltd.

Bhaskara Rao, D. (1982). *An Evaluative Study of the New Science Curriculum at Upper Primary Level in Andhra Pradesh*. Master of Education dissertation, Nagarjuna University.

Bhaskara Rao, D. (1982, June). "Education for Individual Responsibility". *Educational India*. 48: 185-187.

Bhaskara Rao, D. (1983, July). "Teacher : The Supreme of Mankind". *Education*. 63: 193-196.

Bhaskara Rao, D. (1984, February). "Private Educational Institutions". *The Educational Review* XC : 34-36.

Bhaskara Rao, D. (1985, August). "Effective communication in Teaching". *Experiments in Education*. XIII : 109-111.

Bhaskara Rao, D. (1986, February). "Utilisation of community Resources in Science Teaching". *Junior Scientist*. 23: 5-6.

Bhaskara Rao, D. (1988, September). "An Evaluative Study of the Teaching Efficiency of prospective biological Science Teachers". *School Science* XXVI : 17-20.

Bhaskara Rao, D. (1989). *A Comparative Study of Scientific Attitude, Scientific Aptitude and Achievement in Biology at Secondary School Level.* Ph. D. Thesis, Osmania University.

Bhaskara Rao, D. (1989). *Dhrusya Sravana Bhodhapanakaranamulu* (Audio Visual Teaching Aids). Guntur: Nagarjuna Publishers.

Bhaskara Rao, D. (1989, June 24, Saturday). 'Private Residential Coileelu Avasarame!'. *Andhra Patrika*, 5.

Bhaskara Rao, D. (1989, June 25, Sunday), 'Private Residential Collegeelu Avasarame!'. *Andhra Patrika*

Bhaskara Rao, D. (1989, October), "Objectives of Science". *Science Promoter*. 2: 701-703.

Bhaskara Rao, D. (1991, September 16-18). "Biological Basis of Learning". Second International Conference on *Differentiated Psychology of Learning- Its fundamentals and Application*, Martin Luther University, Halle, Germany.

Bhaskara Rao, D. (1992, August 2-8). "Teaching Learning Strategies in environmental Education". *Eights Asian Symposium of the International Council of Associations for Science Education on Science Education for a Changing World.* International Council of Association for Science Education, Colombo, Sri Lanka.

Bhaskara Rao, D. (1992, July 8-14). "Quality or Equality". *Eighth Congress of World Council of Comparative Education Societies on Education, Democracy and Development.* Charles University, Prague, Czechoslovakia.

Bhaskara Rao, D. (1992, May 11-15). "Scientific Attitude in Secondary School Pupils". *Second International Conference on History and Philosophy of Science and Science Teaching*, Queen's University, Kingston, Ontario, Canada.

Bhaskara Rao, D. (1992, October 11-14). "Underachievement : Identification, Diagnosis and Treatment". *Third European conference of the European Council for High Ability on Competence and Responsibility.* University of Munich, Munich, Germany.

Bhaskara Rao, D. (1992, October). "Biological Basis of Learning". *Journal of Educational Research and Extension*. 29: 65-75.

Bhaskara Rao, D. (1993). *Vignanasasthra Bodhana* (Teaching of Science). Guntur: Nagarjuna Publishers.

Bhaskara Rao, D. (1993, August 20-25). "Development of Educational Television in India". International conference Teleteaching 93 on *Learning and Working Independent of Time and Distance.* Foundation for Continuing Education of the Norweigian Institute of Technology, Trondheim, Norway.

Bhaskara Rao, D. (1993, January 3-8). "Teacher's role in dealing with Learning Difficulties". *International Conference on Science Education in Developing Countries: From Theory to Practice.* The Amos De-Shalit Israeli Science Teaching Centre, Jerusalem, Israel.

Bhaskara Rao, D. (1993, November 11-14). "Education for Peace - Need of the Day". Second Conference of the European Peace Research Association on *Improving European Security: Threats and Responsibilities.* Budapest, Hungary.

Bhaskara Rao, D. (1993, October 1-4). "Disarmament". Fifth International Castiglioncello Conference on *Conflicts and Disarmament.* Union of Scientists for Disarmament, Italy.

Bhaskara Rao, D. (1993, September 5-9). "Education vis-a-vis Democracy". Fourth School Year 2020 conference on *The European Educational House.* IMTEC & COMED. Bogensee, Germany.

Bhaskara Rao, D. (1994). *Jeevasasthra Bodhana* (Teaching of Biology). Guntur: Creative Press.

Bhaskara Rao, D. (1994). *Scientific Aptitude.* New Delhi : Ashish Publishing House.

Bhaskara Rao, D. (1994, April 6-9). "Creativity and Academic Achievement". European Council for High Ability's International Workshop on *Creative Potential*-Exploring and Developing, University degli studi di Pavia, Pavia Italy.

Bhaskara Rao, D. (1994, October 8-11). "Special Activities for Talented in General Classes". Fourth conference of the European Council for High Ability on *Nurturing Talent:*

Individual Needs and Social Ability. University of Nijmegen, Nijmegen, The Netherlands.

Bhaskara Rao, D. (1995). *Scientific Attitude*. Ambala Cantt: The Associated Publishers.

Bhaskara Rao, D. (1995). *Vidya Manovignana Sasthram* (Educational Psychology). Guntur: Creative Press.

Bhaskara Rao D. and D. Pushpa Latha (1994). *Achievement in Biology*. New Delhi : Discovery Publishing House.

Bhaskara Rao, D. and D. Pushpa Latha (1994). *Achievement in Science*. New Delhi: Discovery Publishing House.

Bhaskara Rao, D., D. Eliah and G. S. Rao (1987, April). "Pedagogic aptitude of In-service and Pre-serivce Teachers". *The Educational Review*. XCIII : 61-64.

Bhaskara Rao, D., G. S. Rao and L. Rathaiah (1988, September 27). "The Science teacher has a definite role". *The Hindu*.

Bhaskara Rao, D., L. Rathaiah, G. S. Rao and M. V. Lakshmi (1987, August). "Attitudes of Urban Graduate Science Teachers Towards the use of Visual Aids in class Room Teaching," *The Educational Review*, XCII: 133-135.

Bhatia, K.K. (1991). *Measurement and Evaluation in Education*. Ludhiana : Prakash Brothers.

Biswas, A. and J. C. Aggrawal (1987). *Encyclopaedic Dictionary and Directory of Education*, Vol. 1. New Delhi: The Academic Publishers (India).

Biswas, A. and S. Agrawal (1987). *Indian Educational documents Since Independence*. New Delhi : The Academic Publishers (India).

Biswas, A. and S.P. Agrawal (1986). *Development of Education in India*. New Delhi: Concept Publishing Co.

Bloom, Benjamin S., ed. (1959). *Taxonomy of Educational Objectives, Hand Book 1 : Cognitive Domain*. New York: Longman, Green and Co.

Brandwein, Paul F., Fletcher G. Watson and Paul B. Blackwood (1958). *A Book of Research Methods*. New York : Harcout, Brace World, Inc.

Buch, M.B., editor (1979). *Second Survey of Research in Education*. Baroda : Society for Educational Research and Development.

Buch, M.B., Chief Editor (1987). *Third Survey of Research in Education*, 1979-1983. New Delhi: National Council of Educational Research.

Burmester, Mary Alice (1953, March). "The Construction and Validation of a Test to measure some of the Inductive Aspects of Scientific Thinking". *Science Education*. 37 : 131-140.

Desai, D.B. and Ameeta Govind (1979). *Studies in Achievement Motivation*. Baroda : Centre for Advanced Study in Education, M.S. University of Baroda.

Fergusan, George A. (1981). *Statistical analysis in Psychology and Education*, 5th ed. Tokyo : McGraw-Hill International Book Co.

Festinger, Leon and Katz Daniel. (1976). *Research Methods in the Behavioural Sciences*. Amerind Publishing Co.

Freeman, Frank S. (1965). *Theory and Practice of Psychological Testing*, 3rd ed. Calcutta: Oxford & IBH Publishing Co.

Gage, N.L. (1966). *Handbook of Research on Teaching*. Chicago : Rand McNally & Co.

Garret, Henry E. (1979). *Statistics in Psychology and Education*. Bombay: Peffer and Simons Pvt. Ltd.

Gravetter, F. J. and L.B. Wallnau (1987). *Statistics for the Behavioural Sciences*. New Delhi: McGraw-Hill Publishing Co. Ltd.

Guilford, J.P. (1987). *Psychometric Methods*. New Delhi : Tata McGraw-Hill Publishing Co. Ltd.

Jayaswal, S.R. (1968). *Techniques and Tests in Psychology and Education*. Lucknow: Prakashan Kendra.

Kaur, G. (1989). *Underachievement: Identification, Diagnosis and Treatment*. New Delhi: Commonwealth Publishers.

Khanna, S. D., V. K. Saxena, T.P. Lamba and V. Murthy (1982). *Teaching of Mathematics*. Delhi: Doaba House.

National Scheme of In-service Training of School Teachers (1987). *Resource Material, Part 1, General*. New Delhi : National Council of Educational Research and Training.

National Scheme of In-service Training of School Teachers (1987). *Resource Material, Part II, Secondary*, New Delhi: National Council of Educational Research and Training.

Programme of mass Orientation for School Teachers (1988). *In-service Teacher Education Package, Vol 1: For Primary School Teachers*. New Delhi: National Council of Educational Research and Training.

Programme of Mass Orientation for School Teachers (1988). *In-service Teacher Education Vol.II : For Upper Primary & Secondary School Teachers*. New Delhi : National Council of Educational Research and Training.

Rathaiah, L. and D. Bhaskara Rao (1990), 'Residential Collegeelu Vidyarthulni Aakarshinchadaniki Karanalemity'. *Udayam*.

Rathaiah, L. and D. Bhaskara Rao (1990). "Residential Colleges: Relevance in the present system". *The Hindu* : 18.

Rathaiah, L. and D. Bhaskara Rao (1990). "Role of residential colleges". *Indian Express*: 7.

Rathaiah, L. and D. Bhaskara Rao. (1994). *Achievement Correlates*. Ambala Cantt. : The Indian Publications.

Sharma, Radha R. (1985). *Enhancing Academic Achievement —Role of Some Personality Factors*. New Delhi: Concept Publishing Co.

Shukla, U.C. (1977). *Kothari Commission Report*. Lucknow: Parkashan Kendra.

Singh, Raja Roy (1986). *Education in Asia and the Pacific-Retrospect: Prospect*. Bangkok : UNESCO Regional Office for Education in Asia and the Pacific.

Sukhia, S.P., P. V. Mehrotra and R. N. Mehrotra (1980). *Elements of Educational Research*. New Delhi: Allied Publishers Pvt. Ltd.

Sumangala, V. (1988, July). "Effect of Attitude towards Mathematics and Sex on Achievement in Mathematics. *Experiments in Education*. XVI : 156-161.

Sidhu, Kulbir Singh (1988). *The Teaching of Mathematics*. New Delhi: Sterling Publishers Pvt. Ltd.

Walberg, Herbert J. and Geneva D. Haertel, eds. (1990). *The International Encyclopedia of Educational Evaluation*. Oxford: Pergamon Press.

Wanchoo, V.N. and T.N. Raina, eds. (1976). *Research in Science & Mathematics Education*. Ajmer: Regional College of Education.

Appendices

TEST PAPERS

BOARD OF INTERMEDIATE EDUCATION
GOVERNMENT OF ANDHRA PRADESH

March/April 1994

(First year—Year-wise Scheme)

Part III—Sciences

MATHEMATICS—Paper I

(English Version)

Time : 3 Hrs.] [Max. Marks:150

Read the following instructions carefully.

1. *All questions are compulsory.*
2. *Questions from Sl. Nos. 1to 30 are of "very short" answer type. Each question carries one mark. These questions should be answered one after the other in the same serial order. Otherwise they will not be valued.*
3. *Questions from Sl. Nos. 31 to 42 are of "Short" answer type. Each question carries 6 marks.*
4. *Questions with serial Nos. 43 to 46 are of "Long" answer type. Each question carries 12 marks.*

I

1. If $f : R \to R$ and $f(x) = 2x - 1$, write f^{-1}.
2. If $f=\{(1, 2), (2, -3), (3, -1)\}$, find 2f.
3. If $f(x) = \frac{x + 1}{x - 1}$ where $x \neq 1$ find (fo fo f) (2).
4. If $\log_4 (x^2 + x) - \log_4 (x + 1) = 2$, Find x.

5. Express $\frac{1}{(x + 1)(x - 2)}$ as a difference to two partial fractions.

6. Find the square root of $(11 - 4\sqrt{7})$.

7. How many different arrangements can be made out of the letters of the word "MISSISSIPI"?

8. Write the value of $\log_2 3 . \log_3 5 . \log_5 7 . \log_7 8$.

9. If $\frac{3x}{(x - 6)(x + a)} = \frac{2}{(x - 6)} + \frac{1}{(x + a)}$, Find the value of 'a'.

10. If $x = 7 + 4\sqrt{3}$, $y = 7 - \sqrt{3}$ write the value of $\frac{1}{x^2} + \frac{1}{y^2}$.

11. Write the period of the function $\sin(x + 2x + 3x)$.

12. Write the 4th term in the expansion of $\left(x + \frac{2}{x^3}\right)^6$.

13. Given that in Δ ABC, b=4cm, A=45°, B=30° Find the side 'a'.

14. If $(\cos 3\beta + i \sin 3\beta)(\cos 5\alpha + i \sin 5\alpha) = \cos\theta + i \sin\theta$, find θ.

15. Find the value of $\cos\frac{\pi}{20} . \cot\frac{3\pi}{20} . \cot\frac{5\pi}{20} . \cot\frac{7\pi}{20} . \cot\frac{9\pi}{20}$.

16. If $1, \omega, \omega^2$ are the cube roots of units, find the value of $(1-\omega+\omega^2)(1+\omega-\omega^2)$.

17. In Δ ABC, a=5 cm, b=12 cm, c=13 cm, Find r_1.

18. Write the value of $\frac{1}{r_1} + \frac{1}{r_2} + \frac{1}{r_3}$ in terms of r.

19. If x = cis A, y = cis B, z=cis C; (A, B, C are angles of a triangle) write the value of xyz.

20. Find the angle to which the axes be rotated to remove the xy term from the equation, $9x^2 + 2\sqrt{3}xy + 3y^2 = 0$.

21. Find the perpendicular distance of the line $3x + 4y - 5 = 0$ from the origin.

22. What is the equation of the line which passes through the point (1,1) and is perpendicular to $2x + 3y = 5$.
23. Write the equation of the bisectors of the angle between the lines $6x^2 + 5xy - 6y^2 = 0$.
24. Write the co-ordinate of the point of intersection of the pair of lines, $ax^2 + 2hxy + by^2 + 2gx + 2fy + c = 0$.
25. Find the value of k if the lines, $2x + 3ky - 13 = 0$ and $x + 2y + 1 = 0$ are parallel.
26. Evaluate $\lim_{\theta \to o} \frac{\sin a\theta}{\sin b\theta}$.
27. What should be the value of f (0) so that $f(x) = \frac{\sin x}{x}$, $(x \neq 0)$ is continious at $x = 0$.
28. Find the slope of the normal at the pt. (1,2) on the curve $y^2=4x$.
29. Find the percentage error in y if the relative error in y is 0.02.
30. A particle is moving along a straight line according to the law $s=t^3+ 5t-2$, find its velocity when $t = 1$.

II

31. If $f = \{(1, a), (2, b), (1, b), (3, c), (1, c\})$ and $g^{-1} = [(p, a), (q, a), (r, b), (q, c), (p, c)]$ then show that $(g \circ f)^{-1} = f^{-1} o g^{-1}$.
32. Show that $\frac{2}{\sqrt{10+2\sqrt{21}}} - \frac{1}{\sqrt{12-2\sqrt{35}}} + \frac{1}{\sqrt{8-2\sqrt{15}}} = 0.$
33. If A, B, C are the angles of a triangle, Prove that $\cos 2A + \cos 2B + \cos 2C = -4 \cos B \cos C - 1$.
34. Draw the graph of $y = \cos x$ in the interval $[0, 2\pi]$ choosing at least six values of x in the given interval.
35. Solve the equation $\cos 2\theta + \cos 8\theta = \cos 5\theta$.
36. Prove that $2 \tan^{-1}\left(\frac{1}{3}\right) + \tan^{-1}\left(\frac{1}{7}\right) = \left(\frac{\pi}{4}\right)$.
37. Find all the values of $(1+i\sqrt{3})^{1/5}$.

38. Find the equation of the straight line which passes through the points of intersection of the lines $2x-5y + 1 = 0$ and $3x + 2y = 8$ and which makes equal intercepts with the axes of coordinates.

39. Find the length of the altitude from A to the side BC of the ΔABC if the vertices of the triangle are A (5,6), B (1,–4) and C (–4, 0).

40. Evaluate $\lim\limits_{x\to 0}\dfrac{\sqrt{1+x+x^2}-1}{x}$

41. Differentiate $\sin x^2$ from the first principles.

42. Find $\dfrac{dy}{dx}$ if $y = x\sqrt{a^2-x^2}+a^2\sin^{-1}\left(\dfrac{x}{a}\right)$

III

43. Find the sum of the infinite series $1-\frac{1}{8}+\frac{1.3}{8.16}-\frac{1.3.5}{8.16.24}+\ldots$

OR

Show that $1 + \frac{n}{2}+\frac{n(n-1)}{2.4}+\frac{n(n-1)(n-2)}{2.4.6}+\ldots\ldots$

$=1+\frac{n}{3}+\frac{n(n+1)}{3.6}+\frac{n(n+1)(n+2)}{3.6.9}+\ldots\ldots\ldots$

44. A tower AB standing on a level plane is surmounted by a spire BC of the same height as the tower. D is a point in AB such that $AD = \frac{1}{3}AB$. At a point on the plane 100 m from the foot of tower, the angles subtended by AD and BC are equal. Find the height of the tower.

OR

The angle of elevation of the top of an unfinished tower at a point distant 120m from is base is 45°. How much high must the tower be raised so that its angle of elevation at the same point may be 60°.

45. If the lines joining the origin to the points of intersection of the line $x + 2y = k$ with the curve,

$2x^2 - 2xy + 3y^2 + 2x - y - 1 = 0$ are at right angled, find K.

OR

Show that the four lines given by,

$12x^2 + 7xy - 12y^2 = 0$

and $12x^2 + 7xy - 12y^2 - x + 7y - 1 = 0$ form a square.

46. Show that for any point on curve $y^2 = (x + a)^3$ the square of the subtangent varies as the length of the subnormal.

OR

A stone projected vertically upwards moves according to the law $s = 100t - 16t^2$. Find its velocity and acceleration at $t=2$ sec. Also find the maximum height reached.